Blossoming Your Business

A Female Entrepreneur's Guide to Launching Her Own Online Business

Sarah Elfass

Copyright © 2019 Sarah Elfass.

All rights reserved. This book or any portion thereof may not be reproduced or used in any manner whatsoever without the express written permission of the publisher except for the use of brief quotations in a book review.

While attempts have been made to verify the information provided in this publication, author does not assume responsibility for errors, omissions, or contrary interpretations on the subject matter herein. This book is intended for entertainment purposes only. The views expressed in this publication is of the author alone and should not be taken as expert construction or commands. The reader is responsible for his or her actions.

Printed by Amazon, in the United States of America.

First printing, 2019.

www.sarahelfass.com

To my amazing family and husband who always support me through anything, this is for you.

TABLE OF CONTENTS

CHAPTER ONE
THE BEGINNING OF YOUR JOURNEY......1
BECOMING AN ENTREPRENEUR..........6
IS ENTREPRENEURSHIP SOMETHING YOU ARE BORN WITH?...............................9
IS IT REALLY FOR ME?............................12
WHY START TODAY?.................................14
WORKSHEET ONE..............................16

CHAPTER TWO
DISCOVERING YOU............................19
FINDING YOUR PASSION....................21
INVESTING IN YOURSELF...................23
TRANSITIONING FROM 9-5 TO ENTREPRENEUR..............................24
HANDLING OPINIONS OF FRIENDS AND FAMILY...25
WORKSHEET TWO.............................27

CHAPTER THREE
DEFINING YOUR BUSINESS................29
THE PROBLEM SOLVER......................31
NAMING YOUR BIZ..............................34
PERFECTING YOUR ELEVATOR PITCH...37
WORKSHEET THREE..........................40

CHAPTER FOUR
LEGAL TALK......................................42
TAXES AND BOOKKEEPING................44
GET YOUR MONEY GIRL.....................46

BONUS: CHECKLIST..........................49

CHAPTER FIVE
  MARKET RESEARCH 50
  HOW TO STAND OUT AND SHINE 53
  REPRESENTING YOUR BIZ 56
  BRANDING YOUR BIZ...........................57
  FINDING AND TARGETING YOUR IDEAL
  CLIENT...60
  JOIN GROUPS....................................62
  WORKSHEET FIVE..............................64

CHAPTER SIX
  THE BEST SITE FOR YOU.....................66
  LET'S GO PLATFORM SHOPPING!..........70

CHAPTER SEVEN
  MARKETING PLAN..............................74
  DIFFERENT OFFERS & PROMOTIONS...75
  USING SOCIAL MEDIA TO MARKET.......79
  USING SOCIAL MEDIA CREATIVELY.... 85
  CONTENT CREATION..........................86
  GROWING YOUR AUDIENCE................87

CHAPTER EIGHT
  PERFECTING YOUR PRODUCT.............89
  SOURCING MATERIALS.......................92
  HANDLING SUPPLIERS.......................95
  PRODUCT PHOTOS............................98
  PRICING YOUR PRODUCTS.................99

CHAPTER NINE
- *SHIPPING AND HANDLING................102*
- *FREIGHT.............................…..106*

CHAPTER TEN
- *THE BUSINESS PLAN......................…...109*
- *GOALS FOR YOUR BUSINESS.............111*
- *THE LAUNCH...........................…....113*
- *PLANNING FOR THE FUTURE...…....114*

SNEAK PEEK OF BOOK TWO: NOURISHING YOUR BUSINESS
- *POST LAUNCH..............................122*

"BUSINESS" BRAIN DUMP AREA:

Before you start the book, use these pages to have a "business" brain dump. Anything and everything, write it down. Maybe it is some business ideas you have, a problem you would like solved, goals, or anything that comes to your mind. Make sure to write EVERYTHING down. After you have finished brainstorming, start reading this book and get ready to start your journey.

"BUSINESS" BRAIN DUMP AREA CONT.:

CHAPTER ONE

THE BEGINNING OF YOUR JOURNEY

Everything starts from somewhere. Even the simplest beauties of life take patience, dedication, and persistence to grow. Planting a small seed and expecting to grow into a magnificent flower in a day is impossible and unrealistic. You must plant the seed, water it, and nourish it daily. Support it through harsh and destructive weather, shield it from those who seek to destroy it, and dedicate resources solely for its growth. Why? Well, I hope you enjoy flowers, but if you do not, they serve a great purpose. Now, I understand what you are probably thinking right now. "Isn't this book supposed to be about launching your dream business? Learning how to brand, market and have a successful launch?"

Yes, but I always thought of starting a business the same as planting a flower seed. You work hard each and every day to provide what it needs to blossom fully. And even after it blooms, you must take care of it, so it does not dwell. In this book, we will talk about "planting your business seed" and watching it blossom into a beautiful flower, or better yet, your perfect flower. Wow, cliché, right? But it is so true! You want to make sure to have the right tools to help flourish your business. Okay, okay, I promise, no more flower puns, or I will try to keep them to a minimum in the rest of the book. I think you got the idea.

So, welcome to your first steps of opening up the business of your dreams! You might have always had the idea in the back of your head for months, maybe even years now, or you are spontaneous and just thought about starting a business in your dreams last night. You might have a product or service that will solve a problem and help others. If this describes you correctly, then this is the perfect book for you!

I, myself, had the dream of always owning my own business, but was not sure how to start. I went on Google and dived into it, but made MANY mistakes along the way, which is why I decided to write this book. My loss is your gain and would love to help you minimize the errors that you will make. Now, note, I did say you will make mistakes, and that is totally fine! It is how we learn! You learn more from the mistakes you make than from your accomplishments, so do not be afraid to make them and even celebrate them. You might encounter different problems that I have not, but I would love to, if I can, help you through it. In my entrepreneurial journey, I helped many women start their very own online business. As a business coach, I saw women achieve their goals, turn their dreams into reality, with all the tips and tricks included in this book. I know there are many how-to guides out there, but none of them explain in-depth the emotional journey that comes along with entrepreneurship. You will have ups and downs. Some days, you will feel extremely low, not understanding what direction you should take next, while other days you will be on top of the world, feeling really good about your business. Plus, by purchasing this book, you are joining a community filled with amazing women, like you, in your shoes, trying to achieve their dreams.

The journey is a beautiful one. Unlike any other job, you are not following any rules except your own. You get to be your own boss and steer your business in the direction you want to take it in. This journey, however, teaches you a lot. Like, A LOT. It is definitely more rewarding than a traditional job as trial and error is your best friend. You try something; it works; so you keep on going. Now, if you try something and it does not work, you learn from the experience, move on and try something new. I graduated from business school in a good university if I do say so myself (Go Pack!), took entrepreneurship classes during college, and yet I still gained about 70% of my information from the first year of being in business.

Before I dive into the technical parts of launching a business, I wanted to talk about the mindset work behind it. As you will learn in the book, entrepreneurship is not the same as a regular 9-5 job. Making this transition can be tough, which is why I included worksheets that would allow you to take this information and tailor it to you and your needs.

Not only will it be after each mindset chapter, but it will also be up in my Facebook group for your convenience. Just search "Dreaming and Achieving Female Entrepreneurs," on Facebook and a group hosted by me should pop up. This group will have all types of businesswomen, from entrepreneurs who have been in business for years as well as aspiring entrepreneurs just trying to get everything started. We will help each other grow, and by posting your worksheet answers to the group, you can discuss them, ask for advice, and be part of a supportive community to grow and watch each other grow. You will also have FREE access to other worksheets and challenges along with other resources, brainstorming sessions, and even tips from other amazing women in the group to help you achieve your goals in starting your own business. Now, you can just be reading this from the "Look Inside" tab on Amazon, and if you are reading this after you have purchased this book, you're awesome!), which is totally cool, but in order for you to know what is going on in the group, I highly recommend having the book. It will help you understand what exactly we are discussing since we will be going over certain parts of the book more in-depth and referencing it frequently in the group.

Keep in mind; this is just the beginning of many other books as this book only talks about the process from establishing an idea to launching, or "blossoming," your product or service. After launching your business, there are many things you need to know to grow your business called, "Nourishing Your Business" so keep an eye out for that. At the end of this book, you can start reading the first chapter of my second book and continue your journey of starting your business.

So if you are a curious person like me, you are probably thinking, what is this girl's background? Well, I will tell you a little about me. I graduated from the University of Nevada, Reno in 2017 attaining a degree in business management. I remember when I was a senior, taking 21 credits (yes, I was dying, but did anything to graduate in four years!), I had group projects in each class. Literally. Yay for business majors! But I was lucky to meet a lot of people in the process. The question my colleagues were always asking, and basically the only thing they would ever talk about, was: "So have you gotten any interviews yet? Or a job secured after we graduate?" It was fascinating for me to see because I did not try to look for a job after college; I just always knew I was going to be the "next Oprah." Seriously. Ask my parents. I have been telling them that since I was younger and it is still my all-time goal. I decided to try going the traditional route, to say I tried, try to get a job, but realized how pathetic it honestly was. They wanted me to work "entry level" jobs, barely paying minimum wage. I knew that I did not spend over $70,000, four years of hard work and my social life to end up having to work 55+ hours to make $40,000 a year. No, thank you, I'll pass. While it stressed my family out a bit since it is very untraditional, I decided to take a leap of faith and start my own online business, Newni, in remembrance of my grandma and decided to sell the things she loved. I did everything and anything you can think of in the business. I did not hire anyone to help me, so I wore all the hats in my business. From obtaining a business license, designing the packaging, website creation, contacting suppliers, coordinating freight, branding, and everything in between, I have done it.

The point of this book is to get you excited about starting your own online business, or better yet, planting your seed to grow your beautiful flower. Whether it is something handmade you love making or have a unique invention you would like to get out there, there are many things you need to look at to start on the right path.

BECOMING AN ENTREPRENEUR

Entrepreneurship is not like your typical job. It is a lifestyle. You will do a lot of work, but it is entirely worth it in the end because it is yours. It is your flower, your garden. You will be wearing a lot of hats, especially in the beginning. There are many things you have to do at the same time, stretching yourself thin, that it could be overwhelming to some people, but this is not to discourage you, but to prepare you for the journey.

As I said, when I first started my business, it was very nerve-wracking for those surrounding me especially my immediate family, because it was completely different from what they are used to. My father is a professor in Civil Engineering as well as a researcher, while my mother is an accountant. My sister, who just started college wants to go the medical route and my brother, who is 12, has no idea what I do, except that I "am just too busy to ever hang out with him." My husband is taking the speech pathology route, which is also completely different. My chosen path is something way out of their comfort zone, but they have truly supported and appreciated my efforts to start something for myself and chase my dreams.

And so I began. With the little money I saved up from working part-time jobs in college, birthday and Eid money, I started my online store and began taking on orders, fulfilling them and basically did, the whole nine yards. But in the back of my head, I knew I wanted to perform a service. However, I did not think I was "experienced" enough (mistake #1) Yes, I had a bachelor's in business, but what else did I have going for me? (Continuation of mistake #1) To be honest with you though, I am so thankful to be able to go through the experience of opening up my online store, doing everything from scratch and getting no help along the way because I learned a lot! And it led me to paths I would have never crossed without it. That is the journey of entrepreneurship. You are not just waiting for a promotion like ordinary jobs. No, you get to go on different adventures, meet different people, go on other journeys you had no clue that it even existed, and build a background so diverse, no traditional job will ever teach you all of that.

Now, I do not hate on traditional jobs. In fact, they are more stable than owning your own thing, but if you are someone who has always dreamt of owning their own online business, I want you to work on it now. Chase after your dreams, no matter what it is.

Actually, the beauty of the entrepreneurial journey is that you are on this ride, but you have no clue where it is taking you. When I first started a business, it was an online store carrying my grandmother's favorite items, and now, I am helping amazing women create their own online businesses. Interestingly enough, when I first started thinking about this book, it was not a book, but a course. I wanted to create an online course to help people learn about starting a business. One day, I decided with this information, I can create a lot more than just a course, and a book seemed to be the perfect solution for this information. Some might be afraid of this transformation, but as an entrepreneur, it is crucial to understand that this is the nature of the job, but have faith that every experience you go through is an experience, even if it might seem pointless.

IS ENTREPRENEURSHIP SOMETHING YOU ARE BORN WITH?

When I was in college, I decided to minor in entrepreneurship during my junior year. I was unaware of the program, but when I was informed about it, I jumped right on board. But do you ever wonder if entrepreneurship is natured or nurtured? It is fascinating to see the different successful entrepreneurs and their similarity in personal traits, but does that mean it was something they were born with or something they learned?

Being in my entrepreneurship classes, I learned a lot. And because it is definitely different from your tradition 9-5 job, it can be a scary feeling to those who are not ready for the crazy rollercoaster ride of owning a business. Some things you would see in entrepreneurs are the drive and confidence in chasing your dreams. It is a trait you were born with, but something you can learn as well. The drive to get to where you want to be is what will get you where you need to be. Without drive, you will not have the motivation to get up and work towards your dreams.

Entrepreneurs are born with certain traits, but expand their knowledge by furthering their education. Yes, it is excellent for you to know the steps on how to start a business, but without the drive, it will be difficult for you to do it. It takes a lot of courage and self-love to believe in yourself and in your dreams to get it up and running from the ground, and I know you can do it. You just got to believe in it and yourself, too.

An obstacle you might run into, and most likely run into, is the disbelief in your dreams from the people around you. Because it is not your traditional job, most people do not understand what it takes to do your own thing and that is okay. You might get judged, you might get a lot of questions, or even negative comments, telling you "You are not doing a good job" but at the end of the day, you are the only one who knows what your vision looks like. I can try to explain my vision to you for years on end, but you will not envision it the same way I am. The best way to go about it is to disregard any negative comments and show up with your business.

When I was in college, I entered an entrepreneurship competition for $50, 000 to start my own business. All I had to do was to write an in-depth business plan. Sounds easy, right? WRONG! But that was not the hardest part. Honestly, it was the financials. Anyway, I wanted to create a drive-thru grocery store because I HATED having to go into the grocery store to grab a couple of things, especially after work, which is something my mom would tend to ask me to do often (Love you, mom). The drive-thru grocery store was something I wanted to do, and while I did not win the competition, that did not stop me from continuing to make it happen.
Later, I decided to get a mentor, excited to turn my dream into reality and have help along the way to start my grocery drive-thru and, let me tell you,

meeting him for the first time was one of the worst days of my life. The mentors, while they were polite, were crushing my dreams like no tomorrow, making me believe that there was no way I can ever be an entrepreneur. They were telling me that there was NO WAY I can start a business that I had no experience in, like working a grocery store and will never make it. They believed that I did not have any idea or the ability to be a business owner, saying it straight to my face. WOW. I was in complete shock. I went home and just had a meltdown.

Yes, maybe this business idea was not for me, but my drive for entrepreneurship was still there. I wanted to own my own business still and start something amazing, even if it was not a drive-thru grocery store, but the words they told me honestly broke me that day. And it is something I will never forget because that was when I knew I wanted to prove them wrong. I wanted to show them that I had the abilities to do what exactly they told me I could not do. And honestly, I thank them for that. Maybe if I had a different experience with them, then I would have gone through a different path. Yes, they could have been right, but the way it was said is what makes or breaks a person. This is when I realized the importance of good coaching and the idea of empowerment and inspiring, rather than bringing down, which made me explore the field of business coaching and taking this route to help women establish their dream business. No matter what your idea is, know that it is possible for you to do it and achieve your goal if you are passionate about it.

Without passion, even if you have a lot of experience doing it, it will be difficult for you to have it grow.

IS IT REALLY FOR ME?

Okay, so this is something I always hear when I talk to clients. "What if this journey is not for me? What if I am supposed to be a 'traditional' employee and cannot own a thing of my own?" To be honest with you, if you purchased this book, then entrepreneurship is for you. You have an interest in owning your own business. Now, I will not tell you that the journey is an easy one because it is not, but it's definitely a rewarding one. And with this book sparking your interest, I already know that you are already a step in the right direction.

Whenever I meet people and introduce myself as a business owner/business coach, I usually get a couple of responses, "WOW, you look so young, how did you do it?" or "WOW, I always wanted to start my own business, but never did it (or did it when I was in my 40's). Kudos for starting early, having enough time and everything ahead of you to make decisions, make mistakes, and fix them. If I start now or want to start in the future, I will not have time to make mistakes and grow from them," or "That is awesome! I have an amazing idea and want to start a business, but just don't have the time." I was in shock that there were so many people who want to start their own business, but because of family, finances, etc., they are not able to pursue their dreams to take care of their obligations. While I completely understand, it is also essential for you to do what is best for you. As life ticks away, you might not have time to do what you love, so you have to start whenever you can.

But, no, no, no, no. This is soo wrong! It is NEVER too late to start! Start today! No matter how old you are, what you are doing, how many kids you have, your social status, ANYTHING, now is your time to start your dream online business. No matter what it takes. Want to start slow? Sure, but do something towards your dreams. Girl, I get it. We got things to do, taking care of others, providing for our families, but this is the time to take care of YOU. Do what you want to do. Be happy with what you are doing plus, make an income that can support everyone. Why not do both? Doesn't sound like a dream?

It is for you, as well as it is for others. Someone might need your product or service. Someone might be wishing there was something out there to help them, and that is your product. Imagine if Steve Jobs always had the idea of creating an iPhone, but never went through with it? Or any Apple product. You wouldn't have the phone or iPad you are reading this on if you own an iPhone of course. My point is to tell you that you never know what a person wants or needs in their life. Your idea can be beneficial to people, which is why you have to start your business, girl!

Easier said than done, I know, which is why there's an exercise after this chapter for you to fully understand the lifestyle and tailor it to you and your needs. Some questions might seem harsh, but they are things you need to ask yourself. Post your answers to the Facebook group to discuss, get feedback, and even help from others going through the same thing like you; it truly helps!

WHY START TODAY?

I hope by this point, I have convinced you to start researching your idea and getting excited to start an online business of your own. However, if I have failed thus far, I would hope that this section would help you make this decision. Deciding on starting a business can be very challenging. There are a lot of determining factors. To drop your high-paying job to pursue your dreams and not get a return on your investment (especially right away) is tough and can be very frightening. You got car payments, loans, kids and family to support, and even mortgages to pay off. It is definitely a scary thought. But you do not have to drop everything at once to start your dream. In fact, most entrepreneurs start their journey part-time and end up quitting their job once they know they can support themselves with their business. But, hey, they started! And that is the most important thing! We always say we will start tomorrow, but you will not begin achieving your dreams until you start working towards them, even if they are just baby steps.

So, I get it. We are all busy. We all have things to pay off. We all have other priorities. But imagine not going anything that you want or have dreamt of doing just because you're too busy achieving someone else's dream. Have you ever thought about it this way? Yes, they are paying the bills, but eventually, especially if you always dreamed of starting something of your own, you might feel like it is too late to start and never do what you wanted to do, even if it could have helped other people if only they knew about your product or service!

Also, as women, we tend always to put ourselves last. We want to help and take care of our kids, our husband, our parents, even friends first, before we really look after ourselves. We need to start doing things for ourselves. While we can help others, we need to understand that we have to do something for ourselves, too.

While you may not become a billionaire by tomorrow, I want you just to start doing what you love and pursue your dreams. If owning your own online business is your dream, go for it and start today! Start by doing research. Start by seeing what products you would like to sell. Anything. But make sure you start.

Worksheet: Chapter One

Welcome to your first activity! These are here to help you understand each chapter more clearly and start creating a vision for your own business! Be sure to share your answers on Facebook to discuss with other like-minded ladies and get clear answers.

AM I REALLY READY TO BECOME AN ENTREPRENEUR?

Here are some questions you should ask yourself:

1. Why do I want to start my business?

   _____
   _____
   _____

2. What funds are needed to start my business? (Please note we will discuss finances in another chapter but start thinking about what you would need to spend money on.)

   _____
   _____
   _____

3. Do I have a solution to a very popular problem in today's world?

_____
_____

4. If I have partners, how would I divide the business and work? If not, how will I divide my time to stay productive?

_____
_____

5. Do the products we would like to sell have easily accessible materials? Do you already know where you will get your raw materials in bulk? (It's okay if you do not.)

_____
_____

6. Business is all about marketing yourself. Social media is very important to use when creating a business, especially if you will be operating from home. Are you willing to make a plan to advertise and promote your business?

_____
_____
_____

7. Who are some essential people I would hire to run my business?

_____
_____

8. A myth about owning your business is that you do not need to work 40 hours a week. Actually, you have to work more! Is this something you are willing to do?

_____
_____

9. If you can create your dream business just by thinking about it, how would it be? How do you envision it?

_____
_____
_____

10. Am I excited to start my online business?! When am I going to start?

_____
_____
_____

CHAPTER TWO

DISCOVERING YOU

Have you ever really sat down and thought to yourself, "who am I? What is my purpose in this world?" I know I have. And honestly, I get extremely anxious just thinking about it. While I feel like I know what I want to do, sometimes I feel like I am not doing it properly, which scares me even more. I know I want to help women start their own online businesses while being able to juggle my home life. I am living it and could not be happier. But to tell you the truth, it is not as easy as it sounds. My journey to discovering this was a long one, but one I had to go through to learn a lot about myself and what I have to do. Now is your time to learn about yourself because you have a lot of great things to offer to the world;

you just might not have discovered it yet. Something I always hear when talking with clients is that they wish they knew what they wanted to do at an earlier stage in life. They feel like they wasted time trying to figure out what exactly they enjoy doing and this is something most of us go through. But let's try to change this today!

For this assignment after this chapter, I would like you to take about 30 minutes or so just focusing on yourself. No, not what is your role in your family, not what people EXPECT you to do, but what you expect and want to see from yourself. If you had to only focus on yourself, what would you be doing? If money was not an issue, what would you be doing right now? These are just some things you need to think about.

Most of the time, we do things because we are obligated to, not because we want to. While this is the reality for many people, you can always change it if you have a different vision for yourself. I am telling you that you can. As women, we are raised to nurture people around us. We have to take care of our husband, our kids, our parents, and overall, be caregivers. While it is great to care for others, you must be content with yourself and your dream to help others. You will not be able to fully take care of others when you do not know your strengths, your weaknesses, what you can offer to the world and what you can improve on.

Discovering yourself is a process, and you can learn new things about yourself over time, but one you can definitely do.

FINDING YOUR PASSION

Finding your passion is different from discovering yourself. What do you like to do? What would you like to achieve? What purpose do you serve here? All these questions can lead you in the direction of finding your true passion. I knew I always wanted to open up my own business, specifically a service but did not HOW to do it. I latched onto owning my own business and went into e-commerce, which was not my ideal business, but it was a start to finding my true passion. While it may not have been the perfect business for me, it helped me gain the experience and knowledge I needed to be able to create the service I love; assisting women to turn their dream business into reality. Being able to see many different women do what they love and transform it into a business where they can earn a high income AND be with their families is the most satisfying thing in the world for me. While it may have taken a year or so for me to figure out my true path, I kept asking myself, "Is this really what I am meant to be doing? Am I supposed to run an e-commerce store, or is there more to it, I just have not discovered it yet?" Luckily, I was able to find what I was passionate about and start helping women from all around the globe and see amazing results that help me grow and grow each and every day.

Your story to finding your true passion can be a little different but does not mean that you will not reach what your true passion is. Take some time, even if it is while you are exercising, cooking, walking doing something you love, or just lying in bed, to really think about what you are passionate about.

Recently, I was curious to "see" my younger self again and decided to go down memory lane on Facebook. I opened my account when I was about 13 or 14 years old and was VERY active on it, so I got to learn a lot about myself. And let me tell you, the CRINGE. I was saying things that I would never be able to even think about these days, let alone say it, but it was who I was at the time. I had a completely different mindset, and my passion was very different. I knew I always wanted to help people, but I thought the only way I can help others was through therapy and I was planning on being in school forever to become a psychologist. While it is still something I admire, ten years later, I realize I had the right idea, just wrong execution. Yes, I wanted to help people, but not in a "How do you feel about that?" setting but more in a "Let's set goals and conquer this thing" kind of setting. And quite frankly, I am as happy as can be with my decision.

With that being said, always make sure you spend the time to find your true passion. If it means you dive into a couple of different things to figure it out, then so be it. Do many things. Do everything it takes. Do not let fear stop you from doing something, because maybe, just maybe, it can be what you are absolutely passionate about and you would have never known if you never did it.

INVESTING IN YOURSELF

When you think of investments, I bet you the first thing that comes to your mind is property investment, but have you ever thought about investing in yourself? Education is number one, and everything you need and forever will be the best investment you will ever make. The saying, "Give a man a fish, and he will eat that day. Teach a man how to fish, and he will eat forever" is the most significant saying out there. Knowledge is power and is something that you will be with you forever. It will never fade, whereas other investments, like property and other materialistic things, can lose value rapidly over time.

Be sure to invest in yourself. Learn a new skill. Learn a new topic. Take on a new hobby. Always learn new things. Whether it is enrolling in college, taking courses, or even reading books, like this one, in your interest, it is vital to take the value from them. Yes, you can pay, get in a course and read the first couple of modules or pages, but the knowledge you gather from it is what is essential. If you learned to discover yourself, find your passion AND start your own online business, then you have gained an extensive amount of knowledge. Take college classes. Read books. Learn from others.

Now, I hated reading when I was a child. Ironic right? Reading logs were the worst. I would always try to get out of them. But now, interestingly enough, I LOVE books. I can read one every two days (Not too bad for someone who never used to read). I realized it was because of the content. While I know other authors spend a lot of time creating novels for young readers, and the amount of work and creativity that is involved in a lot, I just was never really into them. I would skim them and say that I read so that my mom can sign my reading log. Now, I can read a full self-help or business book and feel so inspired and empowered afterward that I want just to read more and more. Listening to podcasts and watching educational YouTube videos are also great ways to invest in yourself.

Investing does not always mean property or money. It implies in education too. So make sure you are spending enough time and energy to educate yourself on topics in your interest and become an expert if you would like to have it as your living.

TRANSITIONING FROM 9-5 TO ENTREPRENEUR

What a transition! Instead of working for someone else, you are officially your own boss. Now do not get me wrong; it can be horrifying. The perks of being someone else's employee is that they carry the burden of the business. You know you will get paid no matter what, but when you are an entrepreneur, it is entirely different. Some might look at it as a risk, but it is actually a blessing in disguise. Have you ever felt like you are forced to do something a certain way in your 9-5 job, even though you know you can do it better, but your boss is not listening to you? You get frustrated at the fact that you have to do things a certain way when you know you can do it better a different way. And that is completely understandable. You follow the rules that corporate implements and you move on.

For me, it was tough for me to just "accept" how it is and move on. I am a problem solver and honestly, lazy, but you know what they say about lazy people? They come up with some of the most creative solutions, right? But on a serious note, it was tough for me to follow without having the freedom to make necessary changes.

The transition to entrepreneurship is frightening, especially financially, but, again, that is why you can start part-time. Do not quit your job until you feel comfortable. It will be a lot of work, but if you want to open up your own business, it will just be for a while until you can make the full transition and work on your terms, your hours. It will take time, but do not give up. Always chase your dreams.

HANDLING OPINIONS OF FRIENDS AND FAMILY

Fellow entrepreneurs out there probably know what I am about to talk about. As much as it is a touchy subject, it is something you need to be fully aware of it. Because being an entrepreneur gives you the freedom to be as creative and flexible as possible, you will find many opinions coming in, trying to help you succeed. My advice to you is to be open as you might find a great idea from the customer's perspective, but develop a thick skin as my dad would always tell me. Just because someone close to you tells you something, does not mean you need to implement it, but consider it.

When they are supportive of what you do, it makes everything a million times better. Because entrepreneurship is a different lifestyle, there are many people out there who do not understand it completely and sometimes; they think that you are not doing anything. Having friends and family be unsupportive of your dreams can hurt you and make you think twice about chasing your dreams, but do not let that stop you. Instead, take it as a challenge and prove them wrong. They might not understand it fully, and once they see results, it can help them understand better, but it is vital not to get discouraged. Work towards your dreams, always.

WORKSHEET: Chapter Two

In order to know what your passion is and what direction you want to take in life, you must ask yourself the right questions and give yourself truthful answers to truly understand yourself.

1. What is your favorite thing to do on your free time?

   _____
   _____
   _____

2. What makes you happy?

   _____
   _____
   _____

3. What do people say you are good at doing?

   _____
   _____
   _____

4. If I spend my life doing X, I will be extremely satisfied:

   _____
   _____
   _____

5. Sometimes, trial and error are a way for you to figure out what is best for you. What are some things you have done and know you will not want to do again?

   _____
   _____
   _____

6. Ask someone you trust to help you in this exercise. I know that when I talk about my passion, my eyes light up. My eyes light up when I talk about:

_____
_____
_____

7. What is stopping you from pursuing your dreams?

_____
_____
_____

8. To find my passion, I need to do some research in the industries I am interested in. What industries are you interested in?

_____
_____
_____

9. What new things am I willing to do to find my passion?

_____
_____
_____

10. How are you investing in yourself?

_____
_____
_____

CHAPTER THREE

DEFINING YOUR BUSINESS

Now that you have spent some time to focus on yourself and what is truly important, it is time to turn your passion into a business. Sometimes, it may be difficult, but this is when your creative juices need to kick in. Everyone has unique talents, and you are no different. You just need to know how to present them the right way to speak to people who think like you and need your service.

When you came up with the list of your passion and discovering yourself, you might have written a lot of things down that do not come together nor can you think of a way to turn it into a business, and that is okay. Take that list, sit down and think about what you would be happy to do for the rest of your life. Try to narrow it down to one thing through a process of elimination. This is the tricky part. I know because I was exactly in your shoes. I want to do everything. I want to help everyone do everything they want to do. That statement was so vague that when someone asked me what I did for a living, my answer would be so long and confusing, I knew people were confused, which is why I narrowed my business to "helping aspiring female entrepreneurs launch their dream online business within six months or less" Short. Sweet. Simple. And, it gets the point across. I stopped getting the follow-up questions of, "so wait, what does that mean?" It was indeed a defining point in my business and something fundamental for me to go through. It is crucial for you to do this. Every business goes through this, especially when branding, which we will go into further detail in chapter five.

Defining your business is directly correlated with discovering yourself, which is why we spent time doing that exercise. What is your one passion (or thing) you would like to share with the world? Not only that but how can your passion solve a problem that your potential customer has? You can have many talents, but focusing on one topic and learning it in great detail can help you get recognized as an expert in a subject, rather than a general business and that can give you significant leverage from your competitors. Think about it this way. Best Buy and Walmart both sell TVs. They mostly sell the same kinds and right around the same price. If you are in the market looking for a new TV but have no clue about TV specs or how they work, who will you go to for advice? You would most likely choose Best Buy. Even though you might not purchase the TV from Best Buy, they have built a brand of trust in anything technology, whereas Walmart is known to carry almost everything, but might not have the full expertise to advise you on specific TV questions and needs. The same thing goes with your business. You have to become an expert in your field, someone people trust with the information. Clients come and ask me for business advice because they know my experience and know that, even though I might not have personally gone through something like their situation, they trust me to conduct research and advise them with the best advice, keeping their best interest in mind.

Be the expert in your field. By defining your business, you are defining yourself, which helps you build a brand and something people will remember for a very long time, if not forever.

THE PROBLEM SOLVER

We all have problems, unfortunately. If I had a solution for every problem I have ever encountered, I would be the happiest girl in the world. I, personally, am a problem solver. When friends and family, clients even, come and rant to me, my first instinct is to find a solution to their problem. I understand that sometimes they do not want a solution, but a shoulder to cry on, but in business, you need to become the problem solver.

People go to experts for solutions. They have an issue with their car; they take it to the expert, a mechanic, not a dentist. They want to dye their hair or need a trim; they go to a hair stylist, not an engineer. They run out of gas; they go to the gas station, not the grocery store. It is truly that simple. You have to think of yourself as the problem solver, and the greatest problem solver in your field. Establishing that credibility is CRUCIAL when starting your business because right when you think of a problem, you think of that person.

As a female entrepreneur, I was searching for like-minded people in Facebook groups. I come from a small town, where many people do not understand how business coaches work, so I wanted to meet ladies out there who are doing similar things to me and connect with them. After being active in the group for a while, I started to notice the people who were always posting and telling people about their services and their expertise. Over and over I would read their posts about their expertise, which made me trust them. Now, if I ever have a question about social media, for example, I know who exactly to go to because of the connection I have built with her in the group. I am going to get into groups further in the course; however, I wanted to spend time discussing the real importance of building that trust and becoming the trusted person in your industry.

Now, you must know a lot about the topic you want to be an expert in. Not only do you have to research everything, you always have to stay updated with the latest information for when people ask you about current events. Experience is also extremely recommended but can be achieved by taking on projects for trades or even do them for free. You might have studied your industry, but nothing beats experience. Go out there and show off your services for free. Gain that experience and network, helping you grow your business faster.

As a business coach and expert in my field, I must understand and know what it takes to start an online business. People come to me and ask a lot of questions regarding starting a business and being current with the latest business world news is extremely important.

Everyone stumbles across problems, and as entrepreneurs, we love to come up with solutions. I know I do. My brain never stops coming up with solutions if I have a problem. What problem would you like to solve? Has someone already solved it? Can you solve it better? These are all great questions to start with when defining your business. You are NOT here to sell products. You are here to sell solutions. People do not want stuff. They want things that will make their lives easier. Be sure to be the solution to their problem, no matter how big or small the problem might be.

NAMING YOUR BIZ

Wow, okay, get your creative juices going, again, for this one because this is going to be intense, well at least for some. For others, they can choose a name within seconds, be happy with it and move along. Now, I am not saying that you have to come up with a business name within seconds, but I genuinely do not recommend you obsessing over it. Yes, it is essential to think of a creative name, but sometimes, it is easier to keep it simple. That is for you to decide. Simple, but meaningful.

Your business name is your first impression on clients and customers. You want to make sure it is a great first impression, whether it creates curiosity for people to look into your business more or understand what exactly you are in business for just by looking at your name.

When coming up with a name, it is important to understand the industry you are in. Some industries require more of a professional name to it, like "group, consulting, etc." While others can be as creative as you desire. A good start would be to look at other business names in the industry to have a clear picture as to what is expected. After you have looked at it, think of your target audience. Now, we will discuss this further in a later chapter, but try to come up with the "perfect person" for your product or service or your ideal client. What words relate to them? Can you make up a word? You might even want to consider naming it in a different language, especially if you are from another region or something that relates to you and the industry that you are in.

Brainstorming in this stage is crucial. After finding words that relate to you and your industry, try to find synonyms, the same word in a different language, combining words, etc. to see what makes you happy with your name. Say your business name out loud and see how you like it. Does it ring well? Is it hard to pronounce? Is it hard to spell? Ask friends and family to see what they think about your business name. Sometimes, because you know how it originated, you envision it differently than other people. See what their first impressions are. If it is hard to pronounce, many people might not want to explore it more, while easier words get more exposure as it is easy to talk about, etc.

Once you come up with words you would like to use; Google becomes your best friend. You want to make sure that no one else has the same name as yours. Search all social media platforms, trademark registries, websites, etc. to make sure that the name is yours. You do not want your customers getting confused when looking for your business.

One tip I would like to give you is to add something in your name that explains the industry you are in. For example, if you are selling scarves, be sure to put scarves or other words representing it for Search Engine Optimization (SEO) purposes, or the ability to find it when someone searches scarves on Google. When you are a small business, people might not know your unique new name yet, so if you have a customer looking for scarves, they are most likely googling "scarves" rather than your business name. Putting "business name" followed by scarves can get people looking at your business, knowing that you are selling the product they are looking for.

For me, I came up with a lot of names. In fact, too many to count, but they were all different depending on the type of business I was thinking about opening that day. When I wanted to open up a drive-thru a grocery store, I was looking at words that would insinuate that it is a grocery store, but at the same time, create a unique word to do so. Since it was not going to be an entire grocery store, I wanted to make sure that my customers were aware of the fact that this drive-through only carried necessities. Brainstorming took some time. The name that I came up with, after long thought and conversations with my family, was Nessgo, aka Necessities To-Go (Genius, right?) It was a catchy name and something I would be happy if I said that I owned Nessgo.

While this business did not go through, Newni, my other business, was a different story. Before opening up this business, I went to Egypt with my family for three weeks to visit my grandmas. My grandma, Newni, had Alzheimer's disease for about seven years and was getting worse faster than we ever thought. She was the kindest person I have ever met and was so thankful I got to live with her for some time. We used to talk for hours, and because she would forget and I loved to talk, I could tell her the same story five times in a row (especially if it is something I am super excited about) and she will give me an amazing and genuine reaction every time. Being extremely sincere and loving, I never thought of her as my grandma, but more like my best friend, really. She knew when I had a crush on a guy (my now hubby), even met him before my parents did, and was always there for me. Fast forward to after our trip in July 2017; August 10 was the dreaded day that we received a phone call from my aunt, crying, telling my family and me the sad, sad news. Newni had passed, and while we were all distraught, we knew she was resting as this disease was extremely tough on her. That is when I knew that Newni would be the perfect name for my business. Having items that were her favorite to use, I can connect with her and genuinely dedicate it to her.

Okay, side story, but my point is that no matter what you want to name your business, you can do it. All you have to do is make sure it fits your industry, represents you, and something you will proud to be shouting out to the world. It might come to you in a dream, something that you see when walking down the street, or something that you are obsessed with, your business name is essential. Take time to get it perfect, but don't overthink it.

PERFECTING YOUR ELEVATOR PITCH

Pitches. This is what defines you and your business. Pretend you are in an elevator with one of the most influential people in your field. They ask you what you do, and you only have about 20 seconds to tell them while you are waiting to stop on your floor EXACTLY who you are and in an intriguing matter for them to want to learn more. It can be quite challenging to narrow down your passion and business in just a couple of sentences, but it is ultimately your first impression when you meet anyone.

When I first started my online store Newni, I used to call it just that, merely an online store. I would never tell people that I named it after my grandmother because she enjoyed the products that I was selling nor did I even explain much about my business because I did not know what else to say. I had to sit down and think about what precisely the purpose of my store is and how I want to market it to people. I noticed after I would tell people that I owned an online store, they would, understandably, ask the following question of, "Oh, what do you sell?" While it is a hook that I had, it was not an attention-grabbing one, but one that had missing information. Defining your business and being able to explain it to someone within 20 seconds with a new exciting hook that can get people to want to learn more.

Instead of saying, *"I own an online store"* try saying, *"I created a community of things my grandmother enjoyed and found useful in her life, making me want to share it with the world."*

Instead of saying, *"I am a business coach"* try saying, *"I help women launch their dream business in six months or less."*

Instead of saying, *"I sell rope baskets"* try saying, *"I encourage people to use storage items to organize their homes."*

You get the idea. These pitches can grab your attention and keep your listener asking for more information. They are intrigued by your occupation and want to understand, giving you time to explain in more detail about your business. However, the elevator pitch is just supposed to be that, an elevator pitch. You can be as creative as you'd like to get people wanting to learn more and use your product/services. Make it as unique as your business is.

WORKSHEET: Chapter Three

Answer the following questions and post in our group to discuss!

1. What purpose does your business have?
   _____
   _____

2. What is your passion that you can turn into a full-time business?
   _____
   _____

3. What talent would you like to share with the world?
   _____
   _____

4. What problem are you going to solve?
   _____
   _____

5. Has the problem been solved already?
   _____
   _____
   _____

6. How are you going to solve the problem differently than your competitors?

_____
_____

7. What industry/niche are you in?

_____
_____

8. What is your "I help" statement?

_____
_____

9. What keywords are in your elevator pitch?

_____
_____

10. What is your elevator pitch?

_____
_____
_____

CHAPTER FOUR

LEGAL TALK

Oh, legal talk. Definitely not my favorite part, but it is vital to understand the rules and regulations, especially in your state and/or country and industry. There are many rules that you must oblige to, but some level of flexibility as well. Be sure to read up on your country and states laws as this is just general information and from my experience obtaining a business license from the state of Nevada.

Before you start, it is crucial to obtain a business license. I know some people start their business first then get the license, but I do not recommend that. There are various forms of licenses, but since this book is specifically for online work from home types of businesses, which tend to be a one-woman show, I recommend you get either a sole-proprietor license of a limited liability corporation (LLC) type of license. An easy way to distinguish between the two is that a sole-proprietor is just acknowledging to the state that you own a business; however, you and your business are one. Meaning, if worst case scenario, you file for bankruptcy in your business, it hits you personally too and vice versa. You and the business are one.

An LLC makes your business its own entity. Meaning you are not personally connected to the business. Anything that happens to your business will be treated separately. If you do decide to take on a partner, an LLC is an excellent way to go. It gives you the freedom to both be on the license and to both have the same level of responsibility and liability in the company. I have an LLC which allows me to separate myself from the business. If I decide to file for bankruptcy one day, God forbid, will not personally affect me.

However, note, this information is about single person businesses. If you are thinking about partnering up, while I do recommend an LLC, there are different things you can do, which you can find more information about online.

Luckily, everything is now filed online. You can fill out all the forms you need to obtain your business license by answering some questions followed by fee payment and voila! You are officially a business owner! You have your business license. Now that you have your state business license, it is also important for you to get a county one, which you have to file for it after you got your state license. For me, I had to go to City Hall to get it issued. However, it may be different for you. Make sure to ask what exactly you need for it to be a smooth process.

Now, if you are working alone, then you are all set to go. Fees for the first round usually is about $600 for both business licenses for an LLC; again, it may vary from state to state. The renewal fee for each year is much less, and if you decide to close your business, you MUST file for the closure of your business. If you do not, you will be fined. If you hire employees, however, you must apply for Worker's Compensation to receive care should any of your employees get hurt on the job. It is a requirement by law if you have any employees.

If you follow the right steps, you can obtain a business license very easily and quickly, make sure you know what exactly you need to start. More information can be found on your state's government websites. Be sure to read that information carefully before filing for a license and contact a lawyer or check out LegalZoom to ensure you understand the process.

TAXES AND BOOKKEEPING

Now, I am not going to give you legal advice. I advise you to talk to a lawyer and accountant. If you have a small budget, I recommend allocating some of your money to an accountant to get your finances correctly recorded from the beginning. This chapter is not intended to talk about the legalities of taxes but is for you to be aware that as a business, you must file for taxes the same way you file for taxes if you work for someone. Depending on your business license, there are different ways and times to file, so that is when your accountant becomes handy.

The most important thing is to make sure you are up to date and accurate with your finances. You can get in some serious trouble if you file inaccurate information. For everything you submit, make sure you have receipts to back you up. I have a folder on my computer where I save all electronic receipts, invoices, bank statements, etc. just in case you are selected to get audited, you have everything to back up your filing.

Now, I know that not everyone is good with numbers and receipts (literally me), but there are software's out there that can help you stay organized and automatically calculated things for you so when it is time to file for taxes, all you have to do is take the number that they give you and voila! It is really that simple.

With that being said, I recommend using either QuickBooks or Xero to keep track of your records. While you may use Excel, it tends to get messy the more you add entries to it. Since QuickBooks and Xero are accounting financial software, they are programmed to do exactly what you need them to do; track your business expenses and records and keep track of how much taxes you owe. I use QuickBooks Online, which is an easy way to enter the information, even though I do not have an extensive background in accounting. It also comes up with a report that you need to file your taxes in just a few minutes and very easy to use.

Also, it is extremely important to keep up with the latest law and regulations to ensure that you are doing what is needed in the small business world. Requirements are always changing so make sure you are on top of it.

There are always people out there that are willing to help you. If you are just starting and unable to hire an accountant, I recommend that you use the customer service lines that they department of taxation and secretary of state have to provide you with information. I also recommend that hiring an account/bookkeeper right when you can afford it is the most crucial thing because it can save you much hassle, especially if you are not proficient in the financial world. Luckily, my mom is an accountant, so she helped me a lot through the process and practically saved my life.

GET YOUR MONEY GIRL

When starting your business, your first thought is probably, "How am I going to gain the funds to start it up?" Valid question. There are many ways you can start, and ultimately, it is your choice as to which route you would like to take.

Bootstrapping is the most common way to raise money for your business. Getting money from friends and family can be a more comfortable way to start raising funds for your business, but keep in mind, you might not receive much. It is pretty much a donation from people you know and wants to support you.

Second, you can start a Kickstarter page. For those who do not know what that is, it is a way for you to show off your business or project, to potentially interested people, and they have the opportunity to support you by backing your project and giving a donation. Setting it up is pretty simple and can be a great way of getting cash for your business. Just a simple video and explanation of what exactly you need the money for can help you get many people to back your project, depending on the quality of it. You set the goal for collecting money within a set time, and if you manage your goal, you will receive your payment. However, be careful, it is an all or nothing type of deal.

The third way of getting money is by applying for grants. Since the government and many companies are encouraging women to start their businesses, there are a lot of grants out there for women. Depending on the type of business and industry you would like to go into, there is a variety of grants for you. Google it or check out your local Small Business Administration (SBA) Center for available grants.

Lastly, getting investors on board with your company can give you an upper hand, especially if they are not only investing their time but their expertise and connections. Being able to receive these benefits can help you reach your business goals faster; however, you will have to give a percentage, or equity, of your business to the investor, meaning it is not 100% yours. That is for you to determine what course of action you need to take to ensure that you are maximizing your business and your financials.

Getting the funds to start your business can feel overwhelming, especially when starting your business and having the risk of not being able to return it. Starting a business is very risky, but doing your due diligence and creating a very close guestimate to how much you need to fund your business or project. If you are working at home with no other employees, bootstrapping, Kickstarter, or even receiving grants particular to your business can be the best route to go, but ultimately, the decision is yours.

BONUS: CHECKLIST

Keep this checklist with you.

Yearly:

__ State Business License
__ City/County Business License
__ Obtain Employer Identification Number (EIN)
__ File Commercial Taxes

Quarterly:

__ File for State Taxes (Depending on the amount you make, you might have to file monthly.)

Daily:

__ Use Excel, Quickbooks or Xero to Track Your Expenses
__ Save Receipts, Invoices, Etc. in a Physical File and/or Computer File

CHAPTER FIVE

MARKET RESEARCH

You got an idea. Everyone that starts a business has an idea, right? However, how do you know if your idea will work in today's society or if it is an actual need in the community? As discussed before, people do not need more products; they need solutions to their problems. Do I really need a phone? Not really, but it allows me to stay connected to others and easily reachable whenever, wherever (hello Shakira!). If phone manufacturers tried to convince you that you need a phone because it looks cool, while some might be interested, others might not want to upgrade from a landline. However, when they market their phones, they explain the problems they solve, making you interested in the product.

While we will discuss marketing down the line, market research is a tad different. Conducting market research is truly important to understand how to turn your idea into a solution people need. Market research is a way to gather information about your idea. There are two main ways to conduct market research: primary research and secondary research.

Primary Research: Consists of attaining the information yourself through surveys, interviews or any information you personally gathered.

Conducting surveys by going around asking people to fill out for you is the most commonly used as you can give incentives or ask people what they think of your idea and if they see the need for it. Be precise in your surveys, maybe even show prototypes (an example of your product) to people so they can see and feel the physical product. You can also ask people to give you suggestions on how to improve your product like what they would like for it to contain or if it has an unnecessary piece to it.

Another great way that I personally love to conduct primary market research is by asking my followers on Instagram and Facebook for feedback. Whether it is what they want me to talk about next or about a program I have, all input is essential and is considered market research so make sure you consider it. Utilizing polls and sticker questions can help you get a good feel for what your followers and customers want from you.

Secondary Research: This is the type of information you gather from other people's studies, surveys, and any other research you can find on the topic. While it is important to Google your idea and see what people think about it or if there is an important need for it, providing primary research is more valuable when it comes to research, if done correctly.

Google the information, gather statistics, look up competitors, what is being done vs. what can be improved can all be found online. The important thing, however, is to make sure you Google it in many different ways to ensure more reliable information. For example, if you are looking for rope baskets, searching for storage boxes, organizers, laundry hamper, Spring cleaning, tidiness, how to clean and organize, etc. can all give you essential information about rope baskets. Google Trends is an excellent way to see when your key terms were searched the most to predict sales.

After conducting primary and secondary research, an essential part of market research is to know how your competitors operate. Are they successful in their operations? What can be improved? What needs to be done to attract customers to your product, whether it is the physical product or the brand, and the feasibility of making your product better. Sometimes, there can be an industry where the product is not perfect; however, customers are not interested in the advancements of the product nor do they think it is necessary which makes them go for the original and more trusted brand to purchase the product.

From that information, you can understand whom you want to be, your brand, and who your target audience is. When a customer is looking for a product, they usually have a particular background, expertise, favorite products related to yours, etc. Using this information correctly can highly benefit you and your ad campaigns, which we will talk about more in the following chapters.

Overall, market research is fundamental. This step is continuous throughout the whole process of starting your business, and even after you launched. You must keep up with the latest products, latest trends and understand what exactly your competitors are doing and how to stay in the lead. Businesses are always trying to stay on top, and even if you are at some point, another business can beat you and attract your customers. You need to know the ins and outs of your business and industry to correctly engage with your customers and make sure you are spending your money wisely in marketing and the correct product you are creating.

HOW TO STAND OUT AND SHINE

With all the market research you conducted, this is your time to stand out and shine with your business. Knowing what exactly you need to attract and engage with your customers can make people want to learn more about your business, even if you are just starting. People love a personal story and love to know how exactly out make your products, what's your background and how you got to where you are today.

So, it would be best if you buckled down your story. Who are you? What are you trying to do? Why would customers purchase your product instead of your competitors? With more and more people, especially women, are getting into owning their own business, the opportunity to stand out and shine gets tougher and tougher every day. However, it is your job to ensure that you are known as the dominant one in your industry, with all the market research and your special touch added to it. Everyone can sell a product, but how you sell the product is an important part. Being able to speak out and relate with your audience can give you major brownie points in the industry. Creating blogs to teach your customers how to use your product can make them trust you.

For example, about a couple of months ago, I got introduced to a very talented baker on Instagram. Not only does she bake amazing cakes with very creative designs, she always shares the process with her followers on her Instagram story. Personally, even though I do not even know how to bake anything, I am always excited to watch her daily stories creating the cakes she has for the week. Some might think that her sharing her process can make her lose customers because they can just theoretically do it themselves, but as a person who has no talent in baking, I wish I had ordered my wedding cake from her. She built her personal brand around being the expert in making beautiful cakes, even though there are more prominent companies that are national. If anyone asks me for cake suggestions, I would always recommend her, even though she has no idea who I am, but because I watch her every day, I am exceptionally fascinated with her work and genuinely appreciate her hustle. I would rather give her money because I have seen how she works than a more prominent company, which is precisely how you should be in your industry. Be the person whom people refer you to. Be the person who is a leader in your industry. Be the person whom people talk about your personal brand and story as an honest and highly expertise when it comes to your industry.

Being able to stand out and shine comes with a lot of self-discovery, which is why we went over it in the beginning. It is important to be true to yourself and understand your capabilities to ensure that people who are following you trust you. Trust is one of the most important factors when it comes to business. If you have a reputation of being a fraud, people will most likely stay away from your business and would not like to support you. Sounds logical, right? Think of it this way; the average American family has a salary of about $50, 000 a year, why would they spend some of their money on your product or services? Make it worth it.

REPRESENTING YOUR BIZ

So how exactly will you stand out and shine? Yes, you can share your personal story but how will you have people associate your product or service to you? A logo is the first step to having a visual associated with you and your brand, so make sure it is representing you well. A logo that has the elements of you and your business can stick to any customer's mind if done correctly.

Have you ever wondered why most food places incorporate the colors red and yellow in their logo? Red and yellow, according to color psychology has been linked to food and hunger. It makes the customers hungry and associates it with food. Blue, on the other hand, reminds people of the ocean and the calmness of it, which is why most therapy and spas end up having a blue logo or add some sort of blue in their logos.

Since color has a significant psychological effect on us, it is crucial to have on hand when deciding on your logo design. Not only is the color essential but there are different types of logos; one containing the name like Macy's or one that only has a visual and can be quickly known if you see it, like Nike's checkmark logo. Your choice to which type of logo can be difficult, but I would always recommend to my clients to make sure they incorporate the name of their business in there somehow. Just starting your business can be tough only to be represented by a vision so making sure that your business name is in the picture can help you build your brand and maybe in the future, you can refer to your business with just a visual when it becomes mainstream.

Now, you do not need to start out with a very professional logo, especially if you have a small budget. Yes, you can tell the difference depending on your experience, but that is your time to ensure that your business products and services are shining. There are apps, like Canva, and programs out there that can help you start creating and designing your logo to attract your clients and customers without breaking the bank, and rebranding is always an option in the future. However, building up your brand and creating those close connections with your customers is important and they will be there with you throughout your transformation.

BRANDING YOUR BIZ

Oh, branding! Some people find this to be the best part of owning a business, and others just do not get it, which is totally okay. In the end, it is imperative in the blossoming process of your business. This is the reason why people will come and buy from you. What makes your business stand out from others? Are you selling unique products? Are you helping a cause that people want to be a part of? Alternatively, are you simply the cheapest on the market? All these, and many other factors, of course, position you in the market and how you strategize your placement in the marketplace is how others are going to perceive you.

Sometimes, it is more complicated than you think. There's a product you would like to sell, you did your research, and it looks like there is a demand for it and medium competition. However, is that really enough to get your products to sell? I learned that the hard way and the answer is no! You have to understand your position in the market and build your brand around it.

Let's take an example: Take a closer look at Nike and Tommy Hilfiger. Most likely, you already know these two brands and understand their market, but let's talk about it. They both are in the fashion (clothes and shoes) industry, but what makes you shop at Nike and what makes you shop at Tommy? Well, Nike is more of an athletic store while Tommy is high end "regular" clothing store. Now, as established as Tommy Hilfiger is, imagine if they decided to get into making athletic gear aggressively and tried to compete with Nike. How would you react? Would you run to grab the latest Tommy running shoes? Research says no as you trust Tommy as a brand selling high-end clothing and not athletic and the same goes for Nike. They have already established their brand and positioned itself in the market in a way that it would be quite challenging to compete with other markets.

While these are two major companies, it is essential to look at your business the same way, no matter how big or small you are. I came up with a checklist that I go over with my clients to buckle down precisely what they are looking for in their business. I will be sharing it in the Facebook group soon where you can look into and ask yourself these questions.

Before opening up your business, take some time to understand the market you want to get into and how are you going to be unique. Why should I buy your product vs. all the products in the world? People work hard for their money and (most of them at least) like to spend it wisely. Make it count for them to go out of their way to purchase your product.

Now that you know a little background about branding, it is vital to take that information and put it on your business. How do you want people to look at your business? What are you trying to get out of your business and is perceived in a positive light? Is this how you want them to look at your business? These are great questions for you to start getting your brand together and seeing how you want people to look at your business.

Building a brand is not easy. It is not something you will build overnight, but something you will acquire over time. Your brand is your voice and style. As you go along in your business, you will become more comfortable in your own skin, helping it get bolder and bolder over time.

FINDING AND TARGETING YOUR IDEAL CLIENT

Business is a funny world. You can have the most fantastic product, but if you are not showing it to the right group of people, your business might not succeed. For example, if McDonald's is trying to market its fast food to vegan and health conscious/fitness trainers, then the fast food chain will not succeed as it is not the right audience. However, when they understand their ideal customer or target audiences, like children or even people/parents on the go, they will get a much better response and engagement from their customers. They can create advertisements just for those ideal customers.

For those who do not know the terms (and trust me, they are a lot so don't feel bad), your target audience is the crowd of people who have the qualities you think will interest them in your product. For the McDonalds example, their target audience might be parents-on-the-go. Their ideal client is the person with ALL of the traits, making it more specific. It is essential to know both because marketing to your target audience will find your ideal customer and help you reach them faster.

Finding your ideal customer/client seems to be easy; however, it is pretty complicated, to say the least. You have to put yourself in your ideal client's shoes. You need to think like them, understand what exactly they are looking for and in need of. What problems do they have, what do they care for and what they believe in to know exactly what they need. This all relates to understanding and defining yourself and your business. If you do not have a clear path for your business, then it will be the same with your ideal client. You have to have a clear message to get your ideal client. Having mixed messages can bring in customers who are curious about what you are doing, not your ideal customer.

Once you find and define your ideal client and target audience, it is your time to market to them. While we will look into that later, it is essential to understand that it is as important to target them as it is to find them. Your next step is to engage with them. Find out where they hang out, where they socialize, what activities they partake in, what their favorite foods are and even their favorite colors. By knowing what they like, you can easily relate to them and get them excited about your products and/or services.

For example, if you are a talented makeup artist, looking for clients, your target audience is girls who follow makeup companies on social media, go to makeup stores like Ulta and Sephora, follow other makeup artists, comment on makeup tutorials on YouTube, and any person who is wearing a good amount of makeup. It is a great start to engage with those customers, seeing what kind of makeup they are looking at, what are the latest trends, etc. to tailor your business to your target audience.

The best advice I can give you is to sit down and think about who is on the other side purchasing your products. Put yourself in their shoes and get a feel of their lives to have ideas for content creation.

JOIN GROUPS

When I first thought of my coaching business, I immediately went on Facebook and searched for groups that consisted is women in business. I wanted to engage in discussion with them to see how their businesses are going and to learn new things from them, and most of all, see how women across the globe run their businesses. These groups have helped me gain the confidence to grow my business and find a clear direction. Not only did I get to meet other amazing women, I got to ask questions I always thought of, but never really got the answers to them. Facebook groups are great because everyone on there, depending on the group, of course, want to help each other. Whether it is to provide a service for you or share information from prior experience, these ladies are amazing! You can also find your ideal client on there too!

I met a lot of amazing women and got to connect with them on a personal level, understanding their struggles (turns out they are kind of like mine) and also learn how they overcome those struggles as well. The beauty of social media groups is that you can connect to anyone across the globe and learn new things from different people all from the comfort of your own home. Messenger, Skype and other great tools out there allow you to connect with others within seconds and share your knowledge.

WORKSHEET: Chapter Five

1. What did you find when you conducted primary market research?

   _____
   _____

2. What did you find when you conducted secondary market research?

   _____
   _____

3. Did you join any Facebook groups to help you grow your business?

   _____
   _____

4. Who is your target audience?

   _____
   _____

5. Who are your competitors?

   _____
   _____

6. How are you different from your competitors?

   _____
   _____
   _____

7. Where does your target audience audience hangout at?

___

8. What strategy do you have to target your ideal client?

___

9. How will you grow your brand?

___

10. What is your brand?

___

CHAPTER SIX

THE BEST SITE FOR YOU

Nowadays, there are many options for you to start your own online business. Depending on the type of business you would like to open, the opportunities are endless for you to create your best site. There are marketplaces out there that have already established their credibility and are very well known to the public. Customers are most likely to go to these sites, like Amazon and Etsy, to shop for all of their needs and can find your listings on there conveniently. However, by working under Amazon or Etsy, you are pretty much under their rules, meaning you do not have the opportunity to have full control of your business. They dictate the placing of your listing and in some cases, how you package your items, but it can be a great start to get your name out there for people to see your products because let's face it, there are millions and millions of websites out there. It can be challenging to drive customers to your website without spending much money on advertising. By using sites that have already established credibility, that can give you that organic sale without having to spend much money on spreading the word about your business.

If you would like to sell handmade items, like accessories or things that are made at home, Etsy is your place to start. It is the best place to find handmade, unique items made by incredibly talented people. I love unique handmade items which are why most of my wedding favors and guestbook were made from creators on Etsy. My guestbook was from Belgium, my cake topper was from Germany, and wedding favors that had our names engraved on them were made in the United States. I got so many compliments on everything, and they were so rare because they were tailored to me. The cool thing about Etsy is that you can purchase cute personalized things for every occasion and literally anything you can think of with a customized twist on it.

Amazon, on the other hand, is the perfect marketplace for wholesale and private label items, meaning that you get products manufactured under your own personal brand and sell it through Amazon, reaching a broader audience and more target audience. There are two ways to sell your products on Amazon; individual or as a business. If you are selling less than 40 items a month, going the individual route can be more beneficial as Amazon will only charge you $.99 fee, not including other FBA fees except for shipping should you choose to use their fulfillment services. On the other hand, if you are selling more than 40 items a month, it is better financially to register as a business and pay $39.99 a month. Another decision you need to make when thinking about placing your products on Amazon is if you would like to use their fulfillment services or not. Fulfillment by Amazon (FBA) is a way to let Amazon take full control of shipping your products to customers, handling customer service, returns and any problems regarding your products. Your job would be to manage your inventory and reorder or expand your brand line as you please. You would also be in charge of marketing your products, but the tedious part of shipping and handling will all be handled through Amazon.

I, personally, started my business handling all shipments to my customers. The advantage is that you get to choose the packaging, handwrite any note you would like to send to your customer, and have much more quality control on each order. However, it is very time consuming, taking a lot of my time away from the critical part of the business including marketing and research. A year later, I decided to send my products to Amazon, giving me a lot more space in my storage unit (aka my parent's garage). And quite frankly, it saved me much time. I can manage my inventory through the Amazon Seller app and focus my time on marketing my products.

Amazon is always making changes. As I am writing my book, these are the current rules as things are frequently changing so make sure to check out their website and Seller Central before making any decisions.

Lastly, and something I highly recommend is to create your own website. Now like I said before, you will not necessarily get a lot of traffic to your website, but you should have a place where you can list all of your items at your pleasure, without the rules and regulations of other companies, restricting you as to how you would like to run your business. While it might not be your primary source to traffic in the beginning, as you build your brand on the other marketplaces, you will find loyal customers wanting more of your products and purchasing your products directly from your website over time. Having it from the beginning allows customers to know that you are here to build your brand and use Amazon or Etsy as a stepping stone into creating your own online empire someday. It is not something you have to have from day one, but keep it in mind, as you are planning to expand and grow your business.

There are many people out there that have built large shops on Etsy and Amazon to which they do not need their own website to grow their business. The decision of selling on your website or using these marketplaces to sell your products is ultimately your decision and something you can always change throughout your journey, however, try to strategically decide the best route for you and your business beforehand to ensure no loss on the way.

Some might think that having a website, in the beginning, is not necessary, and quite frankly, it is your ultimate decision, especially what your budget allows for. While you can start on marketplace sites and social media, at any moment if they disappear, so will your stuff. Recently, Facebook and Instagram went down for a day, and EVERYONE who was running their business on social media was freaking out. There is absolutely nothing they can do about it, and their stuff is just stuck. So keep that in mind when deciding.

LET'S GO PLATFORM SHOPPING!

Alright, you are getting close to getting your business up and running! How exciting! This step may not seem necessary for your customers, but it is vital for you. There are different website hosts out there for every level of experience, but you have to see what works best for you and your business. I have used Squarespace and Wix to set up both of my websites, but know of others, like WordPress and Shopify, that you may want to explore as well.

Squarespace is extremely user-friendly. If you are a beginner, I highly recommend you using Squarespace. Depending on what you will need your site for, there are different monthly (or billed annually) subscriptions that you can do to start your business. If you would like to open up a shop because it uses many resources, it can be the highest subscription, but there are many things you can do with your site. For Newni, I subscribed to the highest package they offered and was able to set up my store with complete details, have customers create accounts and much more, however, if you just want a website for people to understand your business and what you are doing, then the basic ones are definitely the way to go.

TIP: If you are a college student, use your university email and get 50% off your first year!

Another great host is Wix. While building my website on Wix was a little more complicated than using Squarespace, I, with minimal technical experience or background, was able to figure it out. I found it easier to drag and drop things that I would like on my website on Squarespace. However, Wix has a lot more to choose from. There is an app store where you can download most of them for free and add them directly to your site. If you would like to do more complex things on your website, I highly recommend Wix, but if you are looking for something simple, Squarespace is a great way to go.

There are different hosts out there, but one good host and is little cost, sometimes even free, is WordPress. Depending on your needs and use for your website, WordPress can give you many tools to create a beautiful website, but that also depends on the level of technical work you need to put into it. If you are not an expert in web design, it might be a little tough, but not something that cannot be done. There are many fantastic web designers on Fiverr and other websites that can help you make your website your dream site.

Fiverr is a website where freelancers share their work and their experience with you for a little cost! You can look at previous work, reviews and speak with the freelancer to pretty much do anything you need them to do, without breaking the bank. This is the perfect solution for people that are just starting out and do not have a huge budget. If there is something that you do not know how to do it, or think that someone can do it better, check out Fiverr and see if someone can help you for a low price.

Now, if you would like to open an online store, drop ship, which is the process of selling items that you do not have a physical inventory of, but in communication with the supplier to ship it right out to the customer when they need it, the best option for you can be Shopify. While their monthly rates are much higher than other host sites, it is essential to know that running an online store, especially when that is their only focus, can take up much work and they create many resources for you to ensure significant success in your stores. Shopify is perfect for e-commerce stores; however, if you would like to add more pages, like a blog or even more informational pages, it might be tougher to do that.

Many host sites have free trials. Check it out. See what you like and what you dislike. What templates you like better for you, and the level of work you need to get what you want. The decision is ultimately up to you. Like I said before, the experience of your business is what you want it to be, meaning that the customer will not understand nor do they need to know how you set up your website, so make sure you use something easy for you to use and has all the resources you need to be successful.

CHAPTER SEVEN

MARKETING PLAN

So, we just went over some ways to promote your products and services, which vary from industry to industry, as to which approach is practical. That is for you to decide. Or you can join the group, and we can discuss creative ways to market your products (shameless plug). While it is essential to have your very first promotion well thought of and ready to go, it is important to know how you will continue to market your products. While we will go more in-depth in Nourishing Your Business, in the pre-launch phase, it is vital to jot down a couple of ideas for down the road. Think of how your target audience would love an offer and when will they like it. Will it be during the holidays because it is the shopping season? Or is it a product that is more for Spring cleaning, meaning you will get more customers at the beginning of the year? Being aware of how your ideal client is feeling and what they need is the most crucial step in a marketing plan. You need to know what they want to create. Be sure to be open for suggestions and do your market research to get the perfect product.

DIFFERENT OFFERS & PROMOTIONS

If you think creating your website, and everything else we have discussed thus far, will need a lot of creativity, your offers will need even more creativity, and honestly, this is your time to shine and make your business stand out from every other business out there. There can be millions of people trying to sell the exact same product like yours, but what will make them go after yours? Are you adding something unique to your product or service? Or are you marketing it differently? Think about it. There are many different brands out there, so many websites, what makes you drawn to a specific brand, product or service? These types of questions will help you tailor the perfect offer for your customers. So, let's talk about the different types of offers you can give to your customers.

1. Discount (Sales, Clearance, Money Off)

This is one of the most popular ways people start selling their products or services. There is not one person out there that does not like a good deal. If I know that I saved money when purchasing something, then I am a happy camper, even if it is the original price. See, businesses trick us into thinking that the prices they are giving us are a MAJOR sale when in reality, it is just the retail price with a red sign by it. Since red is a thought-provoking color, it makes the person excited about getting a great deal.

2. Coupon Codes

Another great way to get people into your shop or look at your services is by offering coupon codes. Whether you provide a code for your launch, or for a holiday, the cool thing about coupon codes is that you can easily track them and know which code drove the sales up for your business. For my business, I created one for people who signed up for my mailing list, a birthday one, and for most holidays to ensure that customers knew they had an offer in my store if they needed to purchase presents.

Printing them out on cards and handing them out can be very effective to get to your audience, depending on who they are; however, there is a much easier way to do that. Mail Chimp is an effortless way to send out automated emails to your customers. All you need is to collect their emails, and you got direct access to them, sending them as many codes and offers as you would like.

3. Free Products

Sometimes, people just need to see your products. By giving some away, word of mouth marketing can be used very effectively. If your friend got your product, they could tell their friends, explain how amazing (well, hopefully) and run to purchase it themselves.

Another way you can approach free products is if you have a product that is selling well, but not the other, offer the second product as a free gift to anyone who purchases your first product. That way, they can take a look for themselves and see your product at work. For example, a lot of cleaning and shaving companies do that where they can give you a free razor when you purchase shaving cream or a second broom when you buy a broom and the pan.

4.   Refer a Friend

Lots of services are tackling this one down as it is a great way to spread the word, incentivizing others to market for you by offering them a gift (whether it is money for more points towards their service). Most people have about 20-30 friends and family members. If they refer 15 of them and get 6-10 people on board, that can add up to a lot of people at the end.

5.   Stamp Cards

If your business is a service/product often used, like a coffee shop or eyebrow waxing place, most likely you will use this to motivate you to come back. Usually, they give you a card with 10 spots ready to be stamped. Each time you come in, you hand them your card, and with each stamp, you are one step closer to getting your free item, whether it is a free drink or free eyebrow waxing. I, for one, am a sucker for these types of promotions. I get sucked in, and by the time I should stop going for it, I end up needing only two more stamps to get a free one, encouraging me to go more often.

6. Giveaways

Using any social media platform to create a giveaway is an excellent way for people to hear about your product and share your products with your friends. If someone is very interested in your product and want it, they would be willing to share it with their friends and family and do the tasks you list out for them to do. Now, make sure you are fair when it comes to these giveaways. Using a number generator on Google or making sure it is as random as possible is essential so that your brand is trusted.

7. Social Influencers

This is a great way to get a lot of exposure if you have a larger budget. Getting someone who is a social influencer (basically anyone with a massive following on social media or a celebrity) can be costly, but very useful. They have already built an audience who trusts them, so if they show them any product, their audience would be very interested in trying it out. Depending on the influencer, they can ask for quite a bit. If you know someone who is an influencer or interested in trying to look for some, it never hurts to ask if they will do it for a more budget-friendly cost to you.

There are definitely a lot of different offers and promotions out there to encourage you to purchase a lot of products. Take a look around, especially with people in your industry who are successful and try to see what promotions they are running to get their customers back to their store or to use their services. There are so many creative ones out there, but these are just some of the basics that people who study marketing know of, however the more creative, the better to grab your customer's attention and help decide that you are the best in your industry.

Overall, marketing is important. It is how you are going to tell people about your product and be visible. You need to show up and show what you have provided. People love to buy things and services that will serve a purpose to them. It is something they NEED, or they cannot live without it. Ensuring that your product is a need, and not just a want, helps drive up sales drastically.

USING SOCIAL MEDIA TO MARKET

Social media. There are millions and millions of people who use social media, all around the globe. Can you imagine? From your home, you can reach THOUSANDS if not MILLIONS of people just with a click of a button. But are you doing it? Nowadays, with everyone on social media, it is one of the most effective ways to market. You cannot do it without anymore. But each platform is used much differently, and you need to know the difference to ensure that you are maximizing the benefits when using each platform.

FACEBOOK

Facebook is one of the largest social media platforms out there. With millions of users, Facebook can reach a lot of people, primarily through target advertising. This is the place where you can really show off your product with a longer description, longer video and more sharable content giving more in-depth information about your product or service.

Facebook allows you to create business pages and groups to engage with your customers and audience quickly and easily. Building connections with people, letting them know who you are and what your service or product is, can make a huge difference. I, personally, have gotten clients from Facebook groups that I am in and was able to conduct a lot of market research.

A Facebook business page is an excellent way for you to get your information out there, advertise, get bookings, and even share information about your industry, etc. But just recently, Facebook changed its algorithm where Facebook pages will not be shown as much unless you pay for ads to personal accounts as they believe that people tend to get bored of advertisements (I mean, can you blame them?) and want to hide it from their news feed. Groups, on the other hand, get a lot more exposure since it is something you actually wanted to join and the more engagement you have in that group, the more likely you will have more posts pop up from that group. Being visible through Facebook groups is a lot easier than on Facebook business pages, but both do take up a lot of work to ensure that engagement is high. While Facebook does not like when you advertise your business on your personal account, be sure to share your business page posts to reach a much higher audience.

INSTAGRAM

It is all about the pictures. If your product or service has incredible photos that you would love to share, do it! A lot of people admire photographs and can be more attracted to a product or service if there is an aesthetically pleasing photo of it. You can post shorter videos, Instagram stories and even use IGTV to promote your products and services. Hashtags are also a great way to get your products out there because if someone is looking for something specific, they will use hashtags to see what they are looking for.

Hashtags can seem confusing when you first start using them, but they are actually beneficial. They can help your clients find exactly what they are looking for without much effort. They just have to search up the hashtag or find it on another post and click on it, showing you the thousands of other posts that are out there with that hashtag, which is why you have to have a fantastic photo to catch the eye of your ideal client/target audience. For example, if I use the hashtag #businesscoach, my post will pop up under that hashtag if you search it up. However, you will notice that there are about 3.2 million posts (last time I checked) that used the same hashtag, which probably means it will not be seen by many (unless if they spend a lot of time on Instagram, which is definitely not healthy). My advice to you is to use long-tail keywords like #femalebusinesscoach that has lesser posts to ensure that your content gets out there. Long-tail keywords are precise. Think of it this way. If you are trying to buy a dress online, what would you search up? I am sure you would not just put a dress but rather a description of the dress. Let's say it is a long blue dress with lace details. Now it is specific. Use your hashtags to your advantage by correctly using keywords.

TWITTER

Got a quick thought you just have to share with the world? Twitter is the place for you. With under 250 characters (including hashtags), you can tweet a thought or promote your products. Because Twitter does not have a lot of reading, many people appreciate short thoughts that anyone can relate to. It is essential to use hashtags and make sure to make it catchy. Social media influencers do well on Twitter because they have already established their brand and their fans follow them for them. While it can be a great way to reach a different audience, you do not have the flexibility to write a lot about your company or use many hashtags to get your name out there.

PINTEREST

Pinterest is a different type of social media, and honestly, I was confused as to how it truly works for a very long time, but once I learned it, it is a fantastic platform. Pinterest is more of a search engine than a social media platform. When someone wants a creative idea or looking for inspiration, they go to Pinterest to see what others have done, turning it into a more "Creative Google." It is a way for you to link your products, your blogs, and any services you may have to your Pin Board. Not only do you have your stuff on your board, but it is also important to share other people's stuff to ensure you get the traffic you need for customers to stumble across your information as well. The ratio they tell you is about 80/20, sharing other people's content to yours, respectively. While it may be a scary number, people actually can stumble across your Pins much easier if you have other people's work pinned onto yours. When someone is interested in a product or service, they can spend hours looking up content about it, so they will not skip over yours, they will continue reading it to see if you offer different information. Depending on if they enjoyed your article or not, they may be interested in reading up more on your stuff, connecting with you and even end up purchasing your product or service.

TUMBLR

Tumblr is a platform made mostly for bloggers and people who want to share their written work out with the world. If you have a blog, this is the place for you. However, if you are selling a product, you would be better off using the platforms listed above to connect with your target audience truly.

You can write much longer posts, post pictures and hashtags to each post allowing people to see your work. People might not purchase something right away, but it is a great way to make a good lasting relationship with others.

EMAIL CAMPAIGNS

This is not your typical social media platform but can be an excellent way for you to get your business straight into someone's mailbox. Most people check their emails regularly, while they might not have time to check out their social media platforms. MailChimp is a great way to send automated emails straight to your customers without any hassle. Simply get their emails, create an email with anything your heart desires, whether it is a promotion exclusive to them, a business update, or a birthday coupon, you name it. It makes it easy to get your information across without having to send it to each person and can be scheduled. Another cool feature is that you can schedule posts for new subscribers. For example, if you have already sent out a great email, but just had someone subscribe to you recently, then they can still receive your emails in the order you would like them to receive them, all with only a few clicks. No matter which social media platform you decide to choose for your business, make sure to include email marketing to ensure full exposure of your business.

USING SOCIAL MEDIA CREATIVELY

Burger King recently did something that was incredibly genius. They promoted $0.99 Whoppers to anyone who entered in McDonald's. By having the location on your phone, if the app detects that you are at their competitors, they will send you a coupon for a very cheap Whopper to get you into their doors. Clever right? Wendy's decided to go to Twitter and market their food by roasting as many people as they can, increasing their visibility and having people think of Wendy's next time they are deciding where to grab a bite to eat. They even challenged a young man to get a certain amount of retweets to receive free nuggets for the rest of the year, which he successfully did (he was from my hometown too, so pretty cool).

Social media is a great way to connect with others, share ideas, and grow from all across the world. There are different ways to share your products and services out there, but the platforms mentioned above are the most used. Be as creative as you can to stand out. Be unique and think of creative ways to use social media. Whether it is the way Burger King and Wendy's does, referring friends, or even a way never thought of before, be sure to make it the best. Think of every detail when it comes to your marketing plan and ensures that you have the terms and conditions always in sight to stay on the safe side, especially when conducting a giveaway.

CONTENT CREATION

Content is everything. Did you know that people are more willing to purchase something from you if you provide free VALUABLE content? It's true! Building that trust with you is important for them to look into your products. Did you also know that it takes someone about eight times to view something before they think about purchasing it? So if you post something once, people will most likely not look at it again, but providing valuable information about your products consistently can get you a lot more attention and customers. No matter what you are selling, make sure you are taking the time to explain the benefits of your products. Now, because marketing has changed drastically, posting an ad about your product will not sell. You have to convince your customers of the value that your product provides them.

Consistency is also key on social media. You might not have engagement, which basically means people reacting, commenting, liking on your posts, in the beginning, but do not let that stop you from continuing to post consistently. People can find your stuff at random times and start looking at all your older posts, getting to know you and your brand better. So keep posting, keep commenting and liking on similar people in your industry and create connections through social media. After all, that is exactly why social media was created.

GROWING YOUR AUDIENCE

There are two ways you can gain attention on social media; through paid ads and organically. Paying for advertisements allows social media platforms show your product or service to your target audience (whether you chose it or they can arrange it for you), reaching a lot of people depending on the budget you allocate for it. You can also decide what type of engagement you are looking for. If you are selling a product, you can set it to "Shop Now" where the potential customer can shop for your products with just a click of a button. While you may reach a larger audience quicker, it can drain your wallet a lot faster than growing your fan base organically.

Some tips I learned throughout my journey and have seen a dramatic difference in my social media is the use of hashtags and following people who are in the same industry to build a following. To reach your ideal clients easily, look at your competitors and check out their followers' list. Most likely, their followers are following them because they enjoy their content. By following their followers, you might spark an interest in some of the followers in which they will follow you back; then it is your time to win them over. I would personally send each person who followed me a thank you message and try to connect with them just so that they know it is not just another random person trying to follow them and ghost them, but instead want to build a connection with them. Searching through hashtags also allows you to see accounts you did not see before and to interact with others.

      If you do not take anything out from the book, I want you to focus on this: Please DO NOT direct message random people with your products or services before even asking them how they are doing! I know when I get that message, I do not even respond. It is not nice to your customers and can irritate them, trust me. Start up a good conversation by asking how they are doing, what are they doing, commenting on something they posted on their story, etc. to spark up a real conversation then slowly introduce your excellent products and/or services. However, if you are not a social media manager, try not to spend too much time on social media as it will distract you from your actual business. It can be extremely time consuming and distracting. So make it part of your job and give yourself a set amount of time to explore everything. Try to stay focused on your goal.

CHAPTER EIGHT

PERFECTING YOUR PRODUCT

Throughout this time, you should have been conducting market research, as we discussed earlier in the book, to ensure that you are getting the information that your clients want out there. You might think that something is beneficial and needed, but that might not be the case, and you do not get a lot of engagement on it. So continuous conduction of market research is essential to perfect your product.

After you learn what exactly your customers and clients want from you, you need to work on creating the perfect product. If it is a service, pay attention to all the details to ensure that you cover all your bases and do an extraordinary service, making you stand out from the crowd. Make sure that your

service truly is worth the amount you are putting it out there for and that the value it will give to potential clients will absolutely be worth it to them.
Remember, first impressions are vital; I honestly cannot stress that enough. If a client purchases one of your services and is dissatisfied or does not think it is worth its value, then they will most likely not try another one of your services, even if it is 100 times better than the first one. However, if the first service that your client tried was amazing, they will probably go for everything that you offer as you built that trust with them. I, for one, am a sucker for these types of things, but in product lines.

For example, during the holidays, I was passing by a candle and lotion shop when I saw they had a great sale going on. (40% off, what a steal, right?) I only tried one face mask from my sister before and was truly in love with the product, but never went to get one of my own, until I saw the sale. I purchased another mask, for moisturizing (if you were curious) and loved that product too! I needed a good hair mask as well, so I went back to purchase the only one they had, the banana one (also, if you were curious) and my hair felt AMAZING. I could not wait until the next day to get the shampoo, conditioner and basically the entire line of products. I trusted the brand and each product worked so well for me that I was sure I was not wasting my money and that it was a great investment, and a great sale!

For you, you do not know what service or product your line will pick up first, meaning you have to make sure that all of your products are the greatest ones out there.

While services debatably might be a little easier to make and remake, creating a product, on the other hand, can be extremely difficult because most likely you will need to be in touch with an expert to put your thoughts and creations into a physical product. While you might make a prototype, or example of your idea, at home, you will need a manufacturer to make mass production of them if you are planning to sell in retail or on an online store. Whereas, if you are creating handmade products, you need to make sure you are making consistent products in super high quality. Make sure to get your concept down and ready to go. It can take multiple attempts to make before perfecting it. No product or service will be perfect the first time around, and the process can take a long time, so make sure you start as early as you can.

For me, I was genuinely interested in designing my own rope baskets. I love them and wanted to create a design that everyone would love to have in their homes for being aesthetically pleasing as well as very useful. When I spoke with my supplier, which I will get into more details about later on in the book, I kept sending her my designs, some got approved, others rejected, received samples, changed them up, and the cycle kept going until I came up with what seems to me like the perfect product. I wanted to make sure I was delighted with the designs and something my customers would like.

Taking the time to perfect your product does take time, but you will be delighted at the end if you paid close attention to every detail, not regretting anything. For me, I, unfortunately, did not work hard on the packaging, and because I was in a rush and the hand tags were not going to be made in time, I allowed my supplier to send me my rope baskets without hand tags. This was a significant mistake, but a lesson well learned. Take your time in perfecting your product and be sure to start early. You do not want to miss your selling season because of silly mistakes.

SOURCING MATERIALS

Alright, you got everything ready to launch. Your website, your logo, your excitement to get yourself out there, but what about your product? How are you going to make your product if it's going to be handmade? While you can go to any craft store, like JoAnne or Michaels, to pick up some supplies, in the long run, it can become very costly, and the products might not come in bulk. There are alternatives that you can use to get materials in bulk and for much cheaper.

Ali Express (aliexpress.com) is a great resource to get materials. From plastic bags to pretty much anything your little heart desires, you can get anything you need to make your beautiful products. While this site is more for raw materials, if you are looking for suppliers, Ali Baba (alibaba.com), on the other hand, can be very helpful to create a product, mold, or prototype and have them produced it in mass production. For example, in my store, I sold both handmade products as well as products I got made in China and boy, were they different experiences. Using Ali Express for raw materials can be very easy, and since the websites are familiar in their layout, you can easily use both for your products.

When sourcing raw materials, it can be a little harder to get customized materials, but you can definitely purchase it in bulk for a low cost. Depending on your supplier, you might be able to negotiate or see if they can help you get the products that you need.

On the other hand, suppliers are there to create your perfect product, even if it takes multiple attempts. You will try something, get the sample, which usually is pretty expensive (from China to my place, it was around $80 each time), but is a crucial step to creating your perfect product to see every step of the process. Having a friendly relationship with your supplier can also go a long way, because if you are a loyal customer, and a friendly person can receive more benefits and the right to negotiate more than others who did not spend the time building this type of relationship with them. So be kind to your suppliers, understand that they are from different cultures, most likely and that they are trying their best to understand your language, English, and have a completely different background from you.

Understanding your supplier's culture is extremely important when it comes to negotiating with them. They might take certain vacations or not understand certain things you might say. In college, I took an international business class, and interestingly enough, at the time, I kept thinking to myself, "When will I ever use this class?" Like really? I don't plan on working in an international company or anything, but little did I know that it was one of the most important classes I ever took!

One case we talked about a lot during that class was "Mike and Sally go to Saudi Arabia," and even though it's been a couple of years since I have taken this course, I still remember every word of it. It was a case that talked about two Americans who went to Saudi Arabia to conduct business and negotiate a deal for their business. They decided to take a flight to Saudi Arabia Thursday night to make it on Friday to meet. However, in Muslim countries, they take Friday's and Saturday's off instead of Saturday and Sunday because of the religious prayer on Friday. Because Mike and Sally did not know that, they ended up landing on Friday, not being able to make a deal that day, extending their trip and costing them money.

When they were able to set up a meeting time with the company executives, they had many cultural differences, and they did not understand. For Arabs, it is normal for them to bargain and negotiate over tea, which can seem very informal for Americans. Arabs also tend to have very open negotiations to which contracts are not set in stone perhaps like it is for Americans. My point with this long-winded story that I learned about in my senior year of college was to show that not being aware of the culture you are trying to conduct business in can hurt you in the process. Make sure you are knowledgeable about the culture you would like to conduct business in, how they handle their business, and the ins-and-outs to make sure you do not offend them and maintain a great relationship with your supplier.

HANDLING SUPPLIERS

If you are selling a product, this will be extremely important for you. Services, not so much, but it is essential to know this information should you start your own product line in the future. Now, there are many suppliers out there around the world. They want to create your perfect product for you, produce it, put your logo on it, and get it sold under your business. However, there are LOTS more to it than that.

First, you have to make the decision of wanting to create your products in the United States (or the country you are residing in) or internationally. People typically choose China as their primary source of getting products manufactured since they have massive production warehouses and it is much cheaper to have them made there than in the United States. While I know many people are against foreign suppliers and wanting to help the United States economy and jobs by producing everything here, it can get costly very fast. I spoke with a supplier in the United States and a couple in China before I made my decision and the price difference was insane. Producing in the United States would have cut my margins almost in half, which was too much for my business; however, it is an excellent distinguishing point and selling point for your business. Americans love American made products and are willing to pay extra for them if you have the right target audience.

    A fantastic website that allows you to contact any supplier from anywhere in the world, literally, is called Alibaba. It is so cool because it is kind of like Amazon, but for entrepreneurs and major retailers. It is a secure platform to use and allows you to connect with suppliers through their messaging system, see reviews from other retailers and their experience, and ranking of each supplier to verify their legitimacy. The suppliers I chose were gold members on Alibaba, meaning they have been on it for a while and have excellent reviews. They are also legit, which you have to be careful of scammers, of course.

    My advice to you is to be cautious when contacting suppliers, especially when they are so far away. They know that they are not being watched like a hawk and can take shortcuts when creating your products, so be aware. My supplier was great when we were talking initially, however, right when she received the deposit; she ghosted me. And I completely freaked out. I would call her; she would not answer. I would email, she would not reply. This was not how she was in the beginning before I paid for her. I even called from a different number to see if she would pick up, and shocker, she did but hung up when she found out it was me. I was so irritated and even threatened to reverse the charges and get another supplier, to which she decided she will update me on my products. Luckily, in the end, the products ended up good, but she did not make the three months of me waiting easy. I honestly thought I had made a huge mistake and was going to be delivered empty boxes with the way she was treating me, but prayers helped my case.

Something to keep in mind is that workers in China take about a month off for Chinese New Year. It is definitely a big deal there, and if you plan on ordering products during that time, like I unknowingly did, I found myself pushed back a whole month, so plan accordingly.

Another important thing to know when you are ordering from a supplier, domestic or international, is to make sure you have an inspector, usually from another company that specializes in inspecting products (so that it is not biased) to ensure that each product you are making is the quality you want. Now, this can add to your expense, but it is totally worth it if you are planning on sending it directly to a fulfillment center, like Amazon, without inspecting it yourself first. Imagine sending products to customers, thinking that they are in excellent condition, but they are, in fact, far from that? Plus, it is too late, you have already paid your supplier and is a nightmare trying to figure out refunds, especially overseas. I was planning on inspecting it myself when I received my baskets and honestly did not have the extra cash for an inspector, but man, was it a tedious job going through hundreds of rope baskets trying to see if everything passed my quality control standards. If I decide to do it again, I am definitely getting an inspector next time around. My time was definitely not worth it. You can get someone to inspect a percentage of your products if you do not want to pay them to go through one-by-one, but there is still a chance you missed some of the poorly made products.

Every year, Chinese suppliers engage in an expo around March or April where they share their products, and you get to talk to the suppliers personally, get a feel for them and the representative as a person. You want to make sure you are getting the best product, and sometimes, just speaking to a supplier over the phone is not the same as being face-to-face. This can be pretty costly, especially when starting out in your business, but depending on your budget, it might be an excellent way for you to get your perfect product.

PRODUCT PHOTOS

You know the saying, "A picture is worth a thousand words?" I cannot stress ENOUGH how important it is to take amazing pictures of your products. You might have the best product in the world, but if your image is not high-quality, you sure are missing out on amazing sales. I, for one, prefer to take my own pictures as I am very picky with how I would like for them to turn out, but, there are great photographers out there that can take great photos of your products, for a price, of course. When I ordered my products from Alibaba, my supplier gave me the option for them to take professional photos of my product for me to use on my website, or anywhere I wanted to market it, really. It was for about $50, which was a good deal, and a way to get me started on selling my products, without having to spend time having a photo shoot for them.

If you would like a cheaper alternative, you might be able to find local photographers who are willing to do it for a more affordable price if they are looking to grow their business. You can also look for friends and family who have taken photography classes and know the art of pictures to make sure you get the best images. Lastly, you can even take the photos yourself! Nowadays, cell phones have excellent picture quality, and you can pretty much take your own pictures and use them. I know when you are starting out, budgeting can be an issue for you. You will try to cut the cost in any way you can, but make sure to spend some time and energy in your pictures because, at the end of the day, people are basing their judgments on what to spend their money on, especially when online shopping, solely on images.

PRICING YOUR PRODUCTS

Just when you thought you do not need to make any more decisions, nope! You will always have to make decisions, but this one should be more calculated. Have you ever thought to yourself, how do I determine my prices? Simple question, complicated answer.

First thing, I recommend you calculate how much it costs you to make or manufacture your product. Everything to the nitty-gritty details. Try not to forget anything because this is what you will be basing your numbers off of. Once you calculated it, or your cost, you should mark it up by AT LEAST 40% to make a good profit, which is the money you get to pocket. It is vital to have at least 40% to give you a little bit of wiggle room to create discounts, promotions, sales, etc.

After you have determined the price you need to make a profit, now it is time to ask your target audience what they think. See if they would purchase your product in that price range or not. Not only should you ask people, but you should also search your competitors in your industry and check out their price points. Sometimes, if you are more expensive than your competition and it is an identical product, customers are more likely to shop with them. On the contrary, if your products are inexpensive, then customers might worry about the quality of your items and get discouraged from purchasing it. You have to find the happy medium of what your customers would pay and what can get you a profit.

If you find yourself having a hard time coming up with that happy medium, your cost might be too high, cutting away from your margins. If this is the case, try to find a cheaper, but high quality, an alternative to your materials and work really hard to cut your cost down to get that money back for yourself!

CHAPTER NINE

SHIPPING AND HANDLING

If you are going to sell a product from your house, then keep reading. If you have decided to ship your products directly from the supplier to a fulfillment center like Amazon or any other center, then this section might be a little boring for you. Have you ever received a package in the mail and just thought to yourself, "Wow, look at that GORGEOUS packaging?" Like once you received it, the packaging just made it a million times better? This is exactly what you need to think of when sending out your products. Your product might be fantastic, but your packing can make it a million times better! Remember, customers, want to make sure their well-earned money was spent on something worth it and packaging is a big part of it. Customers like to pay attention to details and see that you put time and effort into creating the perfect product, and packaging can make them feel amazing. Depending on the type of product you would like to sell, you will need something to ship it in. Whether it is a box or a poly mailer, you need to ensure that your products make it safely to your customer. I, for one, love poly mailers and can find adorable ones on Amazon and Ali Express. You can find some that fit your brand, or even get customized ones for you on any packaging company; however, it can cost extra. You can also go the traditional route by using regular poly mailers, but I recommend studying the market and seeing what others are doing in your industry.

Poly mailers are great for non-fragile items including pillows and clothes. If you want to send more fragile products in a poly mailer, place it in a bubbled poly mailer and wrap it for extra protection. Remember, postal services do not treat your products as royalty. They can be thrown, so make sure you are protecting everything because, God forbid, anything bad happens, and your product breaks, the cost of replacing it and an upset customer can be costly. Now, you might choose to use poly mailers because of the small size and weight, allowing for lower shipping costs, while other items, such as boxes, can cost more.

Boxes are mostly used for larger products, such as frames or textbooks, to ensure they make it to the customer safely. With the support of cardboard, you can feel relieved that no matter how much they get thrown around, your product will land in the hands of your customers in tip-top condition, if you wrap it correctly. Trial and error are key in this stage, and it is okay to take the first couple of orders to figure out how exactly you want to ship your products out. Try sending them to a friend to see how they receive it, because, trust me, you do not wish to send it to a customer and end up with a bad result.

Now that you looked into your shipping materials, what exactly are you going to put into your package? Well, obviously the product, but what else? The packaging slip for your customers to see is essential, but most importantly, you should put in a thank you card or gift! Trusting a small brand to purchase products from can be very intimidating for customers, so make sure you have them at ease and smile at them when you send personalized thank you notes to each and every one of them. It might be time-consuming, but it is definitely worth your time to make your customers feel appreciated and the urge to order from you again.

Shipping through the mail can get a little expensive especially if you are using regular pricing. There are commercial pricing options out there from all carriers that allow you to ship your products out to your customers with a fraction of the price and it is fast.

ShipStation is a great tool to use as it can connect to any domain, even if you are using an e-commerce platform to ship out your products at a discounted rate. For just a small monthly fee, you can send out orders (depending on your subscription plan, of course) and they do the rest for you. From creating the shipping label to the packaging slip, it is all automatically done with the little information you provide for them. You can also personalize the packaging slips with your business information to make it feel like a personal gift to your customer. It is a secure platform and has terrific customer service that sets up a meeting with you once you sign up to teach you step-by-step how to do everything. Also, if you have many orders, you can do all of them at once without having to print each and every one manually, it can be tedious and very time-consuming. You can sync multiple websites, for example, if you are on Etsy, Amazon and own your own site; you can sync them all onto ShipStation and complete your orders all in one place for a discounted/commercial shipping rate.

There are other options out there as well that can help you; however, I found that ShipStaton was an excellent tool and a must-have for all small business owners who ship products out to their customers all around the world. If you live in the United States and shipping to customers living in the United States, the United States Postal Service (USPS) is a great way to get your products to your customers for a low cost and lower costs. FedEx, UPS, and DHL are suitable for international shipments. However, it might be a little costlier due to the nature of the delivery.

Shipping costs are calculated by the package type (box or poly mailer), the size of the package, and the weight. Being as accurate as possible is important for your parcels to arrive at your customers in a timely manner. Make sure to purchase a package scale from Amazon, or any store of your choice, with reasonable accuracy to ensure no issues when shipping your products. Also, do not forget the packaging slip along with a handwritten note to make your customer's day. A little thing can genuinely go a long way.

Lastly, something many of my clients asks me about is putting their home address on the package. I completely understand the concern which is why I highly recommend getting a PO Box where your customers can return their products, if needed, and do not have to know your home address.

FREIGHT

So before even starting my own business, I barely knew what the word "freight" meant. I know it had to do with shipping, but little did I know what was actually behind everything. While you may receive a package through the USPS, FedEx, UPS, you name it, when you are purchasing products or material in bulk, things automatically change. There is a different process they need to go through before making it to your place or office.

Domestic transactions are definitely more comfortable because you do not need to go through customs, but because you are purchasing many items, the shipping costs will be a lot more than you ever spent on an online store (even if they are charging an outrageous amount for shipping). International transactions, on the other hand, have a lengthy process, but it is essential to understand. Most suppliers have an option to ship out your products or materials to you through them, having a freight forwarder, or someone in charge of the shipping process, do that for them. Sometimes, however, they do charge more and might not be the most cost-effective option, but it can be easier for you if this is your first transaction. Alibaba, the "Amazon" for suppliers, have started to provide a freight service last year, which is what I used to get my rope baskets. If you are going through another company to take care of your freight, you become the person in the middle, communicating with the supplier and the freight forwarder. Connecting them is essential to ensure a smooth transaction.

After the supplier hands over products or materials to the freight forwarder, the freight forwarder takes the pallet and starts sending it out from the country of origin to your place of residence or business. The freight forwarder is in charge of ensuring that your pallet makes it. Larger pallets and shipments most likely, to keep the costs lower, are shipped by boat, especially if it is coming out of the country and in my case, to the United States.

While customs do vary in each country, I will speak on my experience with customs in the United

States. Once the shipment arrived at the dock in Los Angeles, the freight forwarder was there to receive the items and get it through customs, which depending on your items and what they contain, is either an easy or a laborious process. If your products include batteries, metal, or anything that is heavily regulated, you must have certificates that show that these items are safe for use through testing methods as well as pay customs for them. If your items do not have anything attached to them, you would have to pay a fee (mine was $200) and get it on its way. From here, you can do a couple of things: have your shipment shipped to your house, sent to Amazon (if you are selling on Amazon) or to your place of business. The closer you live to the doc, the cheaper your shipping would cost because they have a semi-truck (again, depending on your items) bringing them to you.

Now, keep in mind, this process can take a long time, especially if it is your first time. When using freight overseas, the products can take up to a month to arrive at your destination, let alone the time to get everything manufactured. It is a long process so make sure you are planning ahead, especially around their holidays.

CHAPTER TEN

THE BUSINESS PLAN

So, some might argue when exactly you should start putting together a business plan. Some say it should be one of the first things you do, while others believe it is the last. I encountered a lot, and I mean A LOT of changes in my business career. What I planned to do when I first started is not what I am doing now, and thankful I did not begin my official business plan. However, I must say, it is EXTREMELY important for you to know the plan for your business. What is your purpose? Why exactly are you doing this? (Remember the questions you answered earlier? They will come in handy now) A business with no direction will not succeed, but also do not think that this plan is set in stone. In fact, even though I have been in business for quite some time now, I still make changes to my plan, and you know what, that is absolutely okay.

A business plan is simply what it is named, a plan for your business. This plan should cover each and every aspect of your business (similar to a Marketing plan) to make sure you have thought of each and every step. This can be helpful because, as you have probably already encountered in your business journey that owning a business is not as easy as it seems. There are so many underlying things you have to do to get it done, and the business plan allows you to think about everything, even if it never crossed your mind. Now, some might think it is unnecessary in general, which I'm afraid I have to disagree because a business without direction is a hobby; however, it is obligatory if you are looking to receive loans.

Banks and other loan places want to know what exactly you are doing and how you are going to do it. One of the most looked at parts of a business plan is the financials, especially by banks and investors because of their interest in your business. Make sure you study your numbers thoroughly and know how much, even if it an educated estimate to get what you are looking for.

While the finances are a significant part of your business plan, make sure you are looking at the other parts, including your strategy and the future of your business. You can always find printable templates online to help you.

GOALS FOR YOUR BUSINESS

Goal setting is crucial. It guides you in the right direction and allows you to have a vision for your business. Yes, we can have short term goals, which are extremely important when it comes to daily planning and executing as we discussed before, but what about your long-term goal. Where do you see yourself and your business in the next year? Five years? Ten years? 20 years? Even 50 and 100 years? Might sound crazy, but having an idea of where you want to be and starting to set goals to get there is a great start. You might have a goal to be known and own your own firm, employing over 300 people. You might not do that today, but you for sure can start working towards that path and start pushing yourself towards that dream. However, imagine if you have no direction, what will you do? Where will you take your business? There will not be a guide for you or your business.

Now, they might seem like crazy goals today and something you do not think you can achieve in a million years, but I am not even kidding you, anything can happen. Never in a million years did I think I would be writing this book for you to help you get started achieving your dreams, but it was always something I wanted to do, and I started with an online store. Crazy how life can take you in other directions but leads you to the right where you need to be.

Set crazy goals, I DARE YOU! But I also dare you to follow through with them. Do not just think to yourself, "One day, I want to become a billionaire" then fall asleep — plan to execute. I don't know how many times I need to say this, but it is so important. You have no idea how many times I get an idea, but because of a lack of planning, it fails. If I had it all planned out from the beginning, it could have worked a lot better. An excellent way for you to work on your crazy goals is by breaking down those goals into small manageable activities. I want to write a book. That can be a very overwhelming goal, but if I break it down to writing two chapters a day, it can be much easier to see the light at the end of the tunnel.

There are three types of goals; daily, short-term and long-term goals. All three models are extremely important to stay productive. In today's world, everyone is busy, but are you staying productive? That is the real question. Your daily goals can include bits and pieces of your short and long-term goals.

Now, you set your goals, but are you really going to do it? This is when accountability comes in. While I understand that you can get distracted, especially when working from home, you must work even harder to make sure you are achieving your dreams from the comfort of your very own home. Set times in your calendar, have an accountability friend, incentivize yourself, or do anything you have to do to get things done. However, no one can tell you how to achieve your goals, that is on you. I can tell you ways to crush your goals, but that might not be the way you work. While I can recommend things that might have worked for my clients or me, you might find other ways that are better for you to get to where you want to be.

THE LAUNCH

So, we are coming to the end of our journey together, well in this book at least. The next edition will help you with the next part of your journey. This is the exciting part; the launch of your first business! Woooohoooo! Now, it can be extremely nerve-wracking, trust me, I know, but now is your time to shine genuinely. Throughout this book, we talked about how and what you should do for your launch, how to blossom your business, but also, it is essential to be calm, cool and collected. Your emotions will be going through a lot, but take this time to make sure you got everything ready for your launch. Your products are up to your standards, your branding is yours, and you are overall happy about your business, that is what's important. What strategy are you using? Will you give your customers coupons? Will you have a launch sale? How will you attract your customers?

This is such an exciting time for you so make sure you take this time to cherish it. Record it, journal about it, or even take pictures to look back and see how much you have grown because I guarantee you, you will learn so much on your journey and change the way you conduct business. For me, I completely changed the direction of my business so seeing the videos I would record for myself in the beginning in my business; it is crazy to see how much my mindset, business, and everything really changed.

PLANNING FOR THE FUTURE

So you launched it. Your business has blossomed. I AM SO PROUD OF YOU! Maybe it was exactly how you imagined it, or it was a little bumpy, but either way, you should be EXTREMELY proud of yourself! This is a great first step; there are some people out there who have been dreaming about doing something like this but have not started yet. So pat yourself on the back for getting this far, but do not stop here. You might hit a bump on the road, but keep going. The rewarding feeling you get of having a successful business usually comes after a bump, so make sure you are ready for it. Create, educate and inspire others with your story, your products, your overall business, and continue to do it to keep your business growing and flourishing. So whatever you do, keep going and sharing your fantastic business with amazing people. Most importantly, keep my part of your journey. I would love to know what you learned and what you created.

Now, the beauty of this book and what my goal was for it, was for it to be a good read, no matter where you are or stage you are in life. Yes, it is a how-to guide, but because of the stories in it, you can pick up a copy, enjoy it, and decide later if you want to reread it and go through the step thoroughly to start. If you started looking into your idea as you were reading it, or you started working on your business after reading it, always keep this guide next to you. If you know a friend, who would love this book and in NEED of it, recommend it to them (another shameless plug). You never know when you will need it and when it will come in handy. Once you are ready to move forward in your business, be sure to pick up a copy of "Nourishing Your Business" to get your guide on how to maintain your successful business. While it is essential to have your flower blossom, you need to nourish and water it every day to support it.

However, please, whatever you do, chase after your dreams. If it is to own your own business, but everyone around you thinks you are crazy, just do it anyway. Prove them wrong. No famous business owner, like Elon Musk or Jeff Bezos, knew that they were going to be famous, and they might seem crazy to the people around them, but look at them now. Always motivate yourself by following successful entrepreneurs. Do not look at them with envy, but with inspiration to be the same, no matter what industry you want to be in and no matter how much money you start off with in the bank. Because at the end of the day, you will build something for yourself and your family that can be your bread and butter, be the life of you and most importantly, create an experience that you love.

No matter which way your business journey takes you, be ready for anything it throws at you. If you fall, pick yourself right back up because you are meant to be an entrepreneur and make the life that you have been always dreamed of.

"BUSINESS" BRAIN DUMP AREA:

Welcome to the end! Time for another "business" brain dump. Again, write everything that comes to your mind, but this time I want you to compare to the first brain dump you did before reading this book. Has your mindset changed? New goals? Learned something new? Launched your dream business? Learned things about yourself you never knew before? Are you excited for your new journey? I hope you are! Please share with us on the group; we would love to know!

"BUSINESS" BRAIN DUMP AREA CONT.:

SNEAK PEEK OF BOOK TWO:

NOURISHING YOUR BUSINESS

CHAPTER ONE

POST LAUNCH

Soo…welcome back! Your flower has blossomed, and now you want to nourish it, I see you. Launching your business was a journey you might have never done before, but I hope you learned a lot and enjoyed it. Every day that goes by, you are probably learning more and more about your business to reach the level of success you have always wanted, just with the right tools. While a strong launch is important to have, you must keep your business' momentum going. You cannot only water a flower until it blossoms then expect it to maintain itself.

If you are purchasing this book, I would assume that you enjoyed the launching process of your business and are looking into how to maintain it, right? It is just as important as opening a business.

In this phase, your business has grown drastically, but your goal now is to ensure there is steady growth. It will be a little different from launching your business but need to work hard in making it grow.

Setting everything up correctly the first time makes it a lot easier to maintain it., but do not worry if it is not "perfect" from the beginning. The great thing about owning your own online business is that you can create changes whenever you want, without anyone telling you not to. When I first started my business, I dreamt about doing everything, even fulfilling orders, but shortly after I started, I realized I was spending too much time fulfilling orders and the need of having someone else do it, whether a fulfillment center or another employee started to get to me. I felt like my time was better spent on marketing my business and trying to grow my brand that I ended up shipping my products to Amazon. While it is great to have the freedom to make any decisions you would like, also note that they will all reflect you, whereas if you worked for a company, the "big boss" would be the one that is reflected. Remember, you are the big boss, so it is all you, girl!

By this time in your journey, you should have tried a couple of things out in trial and error. Some things might have worked out perfectly for you, while others, not so much. In this first chapter, I want to talk about reflection. Because you have done a lot to grow your business in a short amount of time, it is essential to look back and really see those numbers, understand what to improve on, what to change, and what to keep doing, because girl, you know this is your thing, and you can do what you want with it!

Your business is truly what you put into it. If you want it to grow, you need to work on it. The more you put in, the more you get out of it. You already know that because you have been through the journey, but keep it up girl, you got this.

www.ingramcontent.com/pod-product-compliance
Lightning Source LLC
Chambersburg PA
CBHW030013190526
45157CB00016B/2692